# The Principality and Power of Europe

*Britain and the emerging
Holy European Empire*

**Adrian Hilton**

Dorchester House Publications

Dorchester House Publications
Box 67
Rickmansworth
Herts WD3 5SJ

Unless otherwise stated, all Bible quotations are taken from the
Authorised King James Version.

First published in 1997

ISBN 0 9518386 2 8

The front cover shows Mary, beneath a halo of 12 stars, taken from
the stained-glass window of the Council of Europe, Strasbourg
Cathedral. She is shown holding the 1000-year-old symbol of
political unification – the crown of the Holy Roman Empire.

'Reichskrone' photograph © Kunsthistorisches Museum, Vienna

Typeset by CRB Associates, Reepham, Norfolk.
Printed in England by Clays Ltd, St Ives plc.

*'He that is first in his own cause seemeth just; but his neighbour cometh and searcheth him.'*

(*Proverbs 18:17*)

# Contents

# Foreword

The Right Honourable The Viscount Tonypandy PC, (Hon) DCL

House of Lords

This splendid book, *The Principality and Power of Europe*, gives a sound and balanced assessment of the current dangers to the United Kingdom caused by our membership of the European Union.

The consequences of our belonging to a Federal Union, in which we would no longer have control over our own economy, are starkly presented.

Deceit in high places has brought us to our present plight, and it is vital that a united endeavour to get out of the iron grip of European politicians should now be made.

Adrian Hilton has rendered the nation a great service by this well-researched book. It is clear that if we are to prove worthy of those men and women who laid down their lives to protect our right to self-government, we must call a halt to the defeatist submission to Herr Kohl's openly avowed intention to gain by diplomatic intrigue an integrated Europe where Germany is dominant.

Every British citizen should read and digest the information presented in this book.

*George Tonypandy*

**Lord Tonypandy of Rhondda**
Formerly George Thomas MP
Speaker of the House of Commons 1976–1983

7

# Preface

The Europe debate is on-going and far-reaching. There may be much in this book which quickly moving events will overtake, but such unknown possibilities do not lessen the need for a Euro-realistic (some may say sceptic) examination of the issues, stemming from Christian convictions, to balance the Europhile arguments being propagated by many national and influential Christian organisations or their leaders. Whereas some of this book's conclusions may represent personal views, I would hope we may be able to differ in the light of the greater unity we share. Charges of 'anti-Europeanism' become meaningless in the knowledge of the wealth of theological giants which Europe has produced. Wycliffe may have been English, but Hus was a Czech, Luther was German, Zwingli was Swiss and Calvin was French. I offer this book knowing that we owe the Reformation to our fellow Europeans. To accuse me of bigotry or xenophobia would, therefore, be an irrational response. This understanding, along with the many corroborated and indisputable facts and figures presented, will, I hope, cause a thorough consideration of the utter darkness of the principality which holds power over Europe. It is a principality which has warred against liberty, justice and truth for centuries, and once again is rearing its ugly head with a different strategy for domination.

The close of this second millennium is being characterised by a lack of courage to come to grips with questions which are unpleasant and may arouse conflicts of opinion.

> 'Even the Christian Church now speaks its message softly, shyly and without conviction. There is widespread distrust of dogmatism and a preference for agnosticism or free thought.'[1]

In the church and in politics, if such questions can no longer be evaded, they are quietly dropped. Alternatively, unanimity is restored by passing a metaphysical resolution which says nothing at all, or may mean all things to all men. In the age of post-modernity, moral and cultural absolutes have fallen victim to 'political correctness'. The assertion of neutrality and tolerance over what have previously been considered fundamental truths has become a dominating spirit of the age. All creeds, cultures and moral codes are perceived as being equal and should be treated as such – none should be regarded as being superior to the others, and the law should not discriminate between them. Moral absolutes and 'sound doctrine' are consequently perceived by many as being bigoted or overly authoritarian, and therefore a threat to tolerance, peace and unity.

When we speak of politics today, we should firstly define its meaning, since we are dealing with a word which has become increasingly debased, and is often used in a 'party political' context. Bertrand Russell observed:

> 'Politics means obtaining money from the rich and votes from the workers, under the pretext of protecting them from each other.'

If he had tried to define *party* politics, he could not have done better, but the true meaning of politics is to serve the 'whole' – the entire community. When politics is understood in this sense, meaning a knowledge of and duty towards the community, then its pursuit becomes a duty for everyone, and Christians in particular. Acting for the good of society is inherent in being salt and light. Hence this book takes no party political stance, left, right or centre, principally because the issue of Europe transcends party politics and its effects are of great concern to the whole United Kingdom. Whether you are federalist or anti-federalist, Labour, Liberal Democrat or Conservative, the decision which negates the future independence of this nation must be for the good of the whole, and any such Act in a mature democracy needs the legitimacy of an endorsement by the people.

Many other distinguished and knowledgeable Christians have contributed their pro-European books to this debate. In the light of *Proverbs 18:17*, previously quoted, it becomes clear that a one-sided argument may appear altogether convincing. This, in turn, can lead to the firm conclusion that 'a united Europe can, and does, work.'[2] However, the principal issues involved and an awareness of British experience throughout history must also be brought into the light and scrutinised. Only then can people claim to be sufficiently informed to draw a balanced conclusion.

I do not believe that Christians can remain uninvolved in politics, if merely by virtue of the fact that we are called to live *in* the world. In a democracy, our responsibility towards governments also permits an input to those governments, and Christians should always be prepared to contend for justice, truth and liberty. Where these are threatened and the threat goes unchecked, the world will be made all the darker, and the affairs of men made all the more godless. The writings of the great prophets of the Bible are unquestionable proof that God's messengers can have a wholehearted involvement in their nations' politics, sounding the alarm and warning the people of imminent disaster.

God, of course, is and always has been in control. He is ultimately sovereign over all presidents, prime ministers, monarchs and potentates. In a pessimistic, hopeless and chaotic world, He remains sovereign and *'worketh all things after the counsel of His own will'* (*Ephesians 1:11*). Governing authorities exist by His appointment: *'They are God's ministers, attending continually upon everything'* (*Romans 13:6*). They are all subject to Him and cannot therefore claim *all* authority. Our obligation is to *'render unto Caesar that which belongs to Caesar'* – obedience and honour, according to Caesar's rightful position – and to render the rest to God. The powers of state are the means by which social order is maintained, for they are God-given. Our prayers are requested that those in government may righteously fulfil their mandate:

> *'I exhort therefore, that, first of all, supplications, prayers, intercessions, and giving of thanks, be made for all men; For kings, and for all that are in authority; that we may lead a quiet and peaceable life in all godliness and honesty. For this is good and acceptable in the sight of God our Saviour; Who will have all men to be saved, and to come unto the knowledge of the truth.'*

(*1 Timothy 2:14*)

Conflict of opinion is, of course, a necessary ingredient in all political activity, and Christians in a free-speaking democracy will inevitably disagree on many issues. But those who close their eyes to urgent problems, or bury their heads ostrich-like in the sand to avoid disturbing the status quo, are practising a form of cowardice which ultimately damages society. Nothing important has ever been achieved by exalting unanimity or 'peace at any price' above truth, and controversy engendered by truth is not unhealthy. Problems have never been solved by people refusing to look at them. They have a habit of reappearing at the worst possible moment, as the issue of Europe does in the political arena, even on the eve of a General Election. It is much healthier to admit their existence, even if this should lead to vehement controversy, because progress can only take place when difficulties are faced head on.

**Adrian Hilton**

## References

1. John Stott. *Tyndale Commentary on John's Letters.*
2. The Evangelical Alliance's Publications & Resources brochure 1996.

# Prologue

(*Sunday Telegraph*, 25th August 1991)

# Now, a Holy European Empire?

From the beginning of his reign Karol Wojtyla spoke out against the division of Europe imposed by the Yalta agreement. The only major statesman before him to speak in precisely these terms had been de Gaulle, with his vision of a Europe stretching "from the Atlantic to the Urals". The Pope echoed those very words.

PROFILE
JOHN PAUL II

On his third visit to Poland, in Warsaw, John Paul II said that he had come "to cry out before Europe and the world for the forgotten people of Eastern Europe". This was a bold and dramatic gesture. The Pope was insisting not only on the scandal, but also in a sense on the *absurdity* of the division of Europe. His untiring insistence that Yalta was a historical and cultural absurdity had an enormous impact, on the Poles in particular, but also on the Hungarians and Czechs.

Wojtyla also believed – contrary to the orthodoxy accepted by all Western politicians – that the whole Soviet empire, including the Soviet Union itself, was a house of cards, and that once the subject populations could be inspired to call the communists' bluff, the whole thing would collapse.

With the demise of Marxism, and the Christian revival in Eastern Europe and Russia, the Polish Pope is in a uniquely influential position. "The Common European Home" is essentially another phrase for Christendom – to which the Eastern Europeans long to return.

A few years ago, when the Pope addressed a meeting of the European Parliament in Strasbourg, the Rev Ian Paisley unfurled a banner denouncing His Holiness as Antichrist. Dr Paisley's banner was immediately wrenched from his grasp by Dr Otto von Habsburg, a member of the Parliament.

It was a symbolic scene, because Dr von Habsburg also goes by the title of Archduke Otto of Austria. In palmier days Otto von Habsburg would have gone by grander titles still: for he would have been Emperor of Austria, Apostolic King of Hungary and Holy Roman Emperor. One of his responsibilities as Holy Roman Emperor would have been to uphold the dignity of the Roman Catholic Church – which might well have meant that at the request of the Pope he would have incarcerated Dr Paisley in one of his remoter fortresses.

Dr Paisley escaped this fate because the old European order, in which the pope rules the spiritual realm and the emperor the secular, has long since passed away. As Mrs Thatcher said in her speech in Chicago earlier this year: "It is time to recognise, even in Brussels, that the age of empire has passed."

But has it? Or did the farcical scene in Strasbourg have a more serious symbolism than we recognised at the time? For there is reason to think not only that the papacy is gaining increasing political influence in the world, but that the EC may indeed bear a more than shadowy resemblance to a European imperial ideal that has never been entirely forgotten.

Empires have frequently expressed civilised ideas, and inspired loyalty from their subjects. When the city of Rome was sacked by Alaric and his Goths in 410 AD the whole world was horrified. St Augustine – himself a native of North Africa – was grief-stricken at what had befallen the Eternal City. He wrote his greatest work, *The City of God*, to prove that this catastrophe could not have been due to the Romans' having abandoned their pagan gods in favour of Christianity.

The memory of the Roman Empire lingered in men's minds for centuries after the Empire had been extinguished in the West by the barbarian invasions. Charlemagne, King of the Franks, was crowned Emperor of the West by the Pope in 800 AD. He wanted to suggest that the Roman Empire had been revived in his person. In the 12th century Frederick Barbarossa ruled Germany, Burgundy and Italy. He called his realm the "Holy Empire".

In general people thought that the only decent, civilised form of rule was a universal empire. They wanted to restore the unity of Europe that the barbarians had destroyed. The idea survived in the Holy Roman Empire – a name that was finally dropped only in 1804. Even Napoleon, when he wanted to legitimise his rule in France, could think of nothing better than to call himself Emperor, and be crowned by the pope.

And when Henry VIII wished to give the legal grounds for English independence from Rome, he said: "This realm of England is an empire." By that be meant that political authority in England was absolute, and could not be subordinate to any concurrent authority, be it that of pope or of emperor.

We may think that all this is the sound of "old, unhappy, far-off things,/And battles long ago". But the Vatican notoriously thinks in centuries. And in John Paul II we have the most political Pope of modern times. It is in the movement towards federalism of the Common Market, with the coming membership of Eastern European countries, as well as in the turmoil in the Soviet Union, that the Pope may see the greatest possibility for an increase in Catholic political power since the fall of Napoleon, or since the Counter-Reformation.

The Common Market itself started under the inspiration of Catholic politicians – such as Adenauer of Germany, Paul-Henri Spaak, Jean Monnet and Robert Schuman. They were all Christian Democrats. They were all deeply influenced by Catholic social teaching. Few European countries have committed themselves to untrammelled capitalism, because most are penetrated by the corporatist ideas of the Church, and the social teaching of the popes from Leo XIII onwards.

John Paul II's recent encyclical, commemorating the *Rerum Novarum* of Leo XIII, gave only a grudging blessing to the free market economy. The EC Social Charter and the socialism of Jacques Delors are imbued with Catholic social doctrine.

If European federalism triumphs, the EC will indeed be an empire. It will lack an emperor: but it will have the Pope. It is difficult not to think that Wojtyla realises this.

'We do not want another committee. We have too many already. What we want is a man of sufficient stature to hold the allegiance of all people, and to lift us out of the economic morass in which we are sinking. Send us such a man and, be he god or the devil, we will receive him.'

*Paul-Henri Spaak*

Former Belgian Prime Minister,
President of the Consultative Assembly
of the Council of Europe, 1949–51

# Chapter 1

## The Vision of the Union

*'And the ten horns which thou sawest are ten kings.'*
(*Revelation 17:12*)

The fighting in Europe finally stopped in the spring of 1945. Never had war been more destructive. The human and material costs were incalculable – more than 40 million dead and a European continent in ruins. This may have been Europe at rock bottom, but it followed the pattern of history: catastrophe, followed by revival, followed by catastrophe. Since the fall of the Roman Empire, there have been numerous attempts to rebuild a unified Europe. The vision of one Empire under one Emperor, belonging to one Church under one God, has caused more bloodshed than anything in the history of the world. Somehow, Europe seemed doomed to oscillate between war and peace, between power and ignominy, between order and chaos.

### A United States of Europe

Winston Churchill suggested a possible solution during a celebrated speech in Zurich, Switzerland, in September 1946:

'We must build a kind of United States of Europe.'

He was not advocating the development of an undemocratic federal superstate, but reiterating the age-old vision of a peacefully unified continent. The devastation of two world wars had made the limitations of national sovereignty painfully evident to many of Europe's leaders. They believed there was an urgent need for a European supranationalism to drown out Europe's individual nationalisms. By instigating an inexorable move to create a family of nations, individual enmities could be laid to rest. Churchill was sure that the primary building block had to be a new partnership between France and Germany. The recreation of the old Empire of Charlemagne was an essential cornerstone of peace in post-war Europe. Therefore, the *Treaty of Paris* in 1951, which created the European Coal and Steel Community (ECSC), bound the French and German economic destinies irrevocably together. The pooling of iron, coal and steel resources was later enlarged to include Italy, Belgium, the Netherlands and Luxembourg.

The Fathers of the emerging empire soon realised that Europe's economic influence in the world would be greatly enhanced by a further weakening of its internal barriers. The *Treaty of Rome*, signed in 1957, brought the European Economic Community (EEC) into being, with the initial goal of removing trade and economic barriers between member states and unifying their economic policies. The ultimate goal, of course, was the eventual political unification of Europe – 'an ever closer union'.[1] By this, the age-old vision of past potentates continued.

## The ancient Empire

Following the early centuries AD, Mediterranean Christianity developed into a series of cults and heresies, with only a small remnant adhering to sound doctrine. As successive Caesars continued to persecute believers for refusing to acknowledge the deification of the emperor, and to sacrifice at his altar, the extreme western portion of the Roman Empire became the place of refuge. Constantius Chlorus was the military ruler of Gaul, Spain and Britain. He prevented the execution of Christians in his region essentially because he esteemed their virtues. His sudden death resulted in his son, Constantine, being declared emperor, though there followed numerous civil wars among rival pretenders for imperial power. By this time, the bishop of Rome had come to be generally acknowledged as the leader of Christianity in the West, and was called 'pope' (from the Latin *'papa'*, meaning father). This title was commonly given to many bishops and it was not until the 9th century that the title was reserved exclusively for the bishop of Rome. Constantine's military supremacy could have been capped by the execution of Rome's Christian leader, but a vision of a flaming cross in the sky convinced him that it was in the name of the Christian God that he had been victorious. Constantine became the first Roman Emperor to profess Christianity, and for the first time in the Empire, Christians were free to practise their religion.

Many believers puzzled over this new order. For nearly three centuries they had waited for the return of Jesus Christ as king and deliverer, the fall of Rome, and the triumph of the kingdom of God. Curiously, no prophecy had foretold a popular growth and universal acceptance of the Church. They saw prophecies of persecution and suffering, but nowhere was the Church of Christ prophesied to become great and powerful in this world. On the contrary, Jesus had said his kingdom was not of this worldly order, and talked much of the world and the Church being at odds until his return. It was not until Constantine began a process of syncretism that Christians began to understand the nature of the beast which was evolving. The Saturday Jewish Sabbath was replaced by Constantine's edict forbidding work on 'the venerable day of the sun' (Sunday), and the celebration of the Passover was declared illegal – on pain of death. It was replaced by 'Easter', celebrated on a Sunday and inherited from a Babylonian cult to the goddess Ishtar. The Roman pseudo-Christianity caused many faithful believers to flee into the mountains of Europe and Asia Minor to escape persecution and death, and there they continued, away from the world's view, as the true church of Christ.

The majority of Christians, however, were awed by the universal influence of the new unity. There was one Empire under one Emperor, leading one Church under one God. Many believers began to wonder if they had not misunderstood the concept of the kingdom of God – it might have been the Church itself, or even the christianised Empire. Thus the fateful union of Church and State was ratified – a union that was to shape the evolution of Europe for centuries to come.

In 337, Constantine died, leaving the Empire to a series of successors. Some, like Julian (the Apostate) hated Christians and tried to revive the old gods. Others, like Theodosius, formally outlawed the old gods and made conversion to Roman Christianity compulsory. He was the last ruler of a united Roman Empire. At his death in 395, the Empire was divided between his two sons. Thus, Eastern Europe pursued a course independently of Western Europe – a separation which was to prove permanent. The Gothic and Germanic tribes effectively conquered the Western Roman Empire in 410, leaving a ceremonial emperor on the imperial throne, and half the Empire occupied by the warring barbarian tribes of Gaul, the Germanic Visigoths and the non-Germanic Hun. These powers seem to have embodied the forces from which Western Europe has never been free.

Pope Leo's intervention to persuade Attila the Hun not to invade Rome was crucial in augmenting the power of the Roman Church and laying the foundation of the temporal power of the popes. It was thus that the primacy of Rome's bishop was asserted over all other bishops. As the Council of Chalcedon stated in 451:

> 'Peter has spoken by Leo; let him be anathema who believes otherwise.'

From this, the doctrine that papal power was granted by Christ to Peter, and that power was passed on by Peter to his successors, began to take firm root. But the Western Empire had merely become a ceremonial show for various Germanic generals, and even that ended in 476, when the final Emperor was deposed, leaving Germanic kings governing every portion. Effectively, the Western Empire had fallen, but forces were already at work to mould a new Roman Empire out of the ruins. As the ancient age drew to a close, the Middle Ages began, with the rising Eastern Empire centred in Constantinople. This city (formerly known as Byzantium) was founded by Constantine in 327 as the new capital of the Eastern half of the Empire. After the fall of Rome, Constantinople and its emperors carried on the traditions of Roman civilisation with one dream – the recovery of the Western provinces and the restoration of the Roman Empire to its full ancient grandeur.

In 554, the Emperor Justinian succeeded in that restoration. He saw himself as God's agent, destroying barbarian heretics, winning back the lost provinces of the West, and healing the divisions inflicted on Rome by barbarian invaders in 476. He acknowledged the supremacy of the Pope in the West, and effectively restored both 'legs' of the Empire – East and West. This became known as the 'Imperial Restoration'. At Justinian's death in 565, the resources of the restored Empire had been depleted and subsequent invasions once again divided East and West for a further two centuries. But the principal focus shifted to the West, as Papal Rome turned its eyes to the powerful Frankish, German and Austrian kings at the heart of Europe.

## The Middle Ages

In AD 800, Charlemagne (Charles the Great), a zealous Roman Catholic, was crowned *Imperator Romanorum* (Emperor of the Romans) by Pope Leo III. He became Western Europe's 'Christian' Caesar – a Roman emperor born of a Germanic race. The West once again had an emperor, and his coronation was to become the central event of the Middle Ages. He was proclaimed *Rex Pater Europae* (King Father of Europe) and espoused the ideal of a unified Christian Empire – albeit christianised at swordpoint – in close alliance with the Pope. The fact that Charlemagne received his crown from the Pope was seen by the populace as equal to a divine bestowal. It confirmed the perception that the imperial crown was a papal gift, and that the kingdoms of this earth belonged to the Bishop of Rome; they were his to give, and his to take away. It was the lesser person being blessed by the greater. According to *Hebrews 7:7*, the person performing the blessing must be the superior party:

> *'And without all contradiction the less is blessed by the better.'*

By this, there had been a formal linking of the Pope's spiritual power with the Emperor's temporal power, and the two had become joint sovereigns on earth, in a Holy Roman Empire which was the political foundation of the Middle Ages. Throughout this era, the memory of the once-great Roman Empire lived as a vital tradition in the hearts of many Europeans. The entire future of the Continent was bound up in this coronation, and the alliance between the papacy and Germany has been of great significance ever since.

Following Charlemagne's death in 814, the cycle of revival followed by disintegration was repeated, and Europe crumbled into feudal states and political mayhem. The *Treaty of Verdun* was agreed between Charlemagne's quarrelsome grandsons in 843. It partitioned the Empire into three, foreshadowing the modern geography of Western Europe. The Holy See was also torn by factionalism, the papacy being bought, sold, and occasionally obtained by murder. The weakness and disunity in the Roman Church was closely reflected in the disunity and chaos throughout Europe.

In 962, Otto the Great revived Charlemagne's Empire as the first German Reich (Empire) and was crowned Holy Roman Emperor by Pope John XII, under whom the Lateran Palace had become a literal brothel. This Reich became known as the *Sacrum Romanum Imperium Nationis Germanicae* (Holy Roman Empire of the German Nation) and Otto's octagonal crown became the symbol of the concept of European unity. Germany became the power centre of the Empire. Throughout the Middle Ages it was to be the kings of the Germans, crowned by the Pope, who would be named Holy Roman Emperor. Otto's death heralded further instability. Old alliances between Emperors and Popes collapsed. The final schism between the Western (Roman) and Eastern (Orthodox) churches was formalised when the Pope at Rome and the Patriarch of Constantinople excommunicated each other. The great medieval struggle between Empire and Papacy was initiated in 1059, when Pope Nicholas II removed the Emperor's influence in Papal elections, sparking a major rupture between Germany and Rome. After the ensuing centuries of German demise and a period without an Emperor, the imperial crown was revived and given to the Austrian Count Rudolf of Habsburg – a name which was to play a leading role in European affairs for centuries to come. Western Europe developed a secular authority, and Papal powers were greatly diminished. French and German tensions resulted in there being two Popes, each denouncing the other as the

Antichrist, and expedience determined which European state supported which Pope. By 1409 there were three Popes, creating an intolerable situation which resulted in a devastating loss of prestige for the Roman Catholic Church.

## The evolution of the Empire

During the 15th and 16th centuries, the Habsburgs had been carefully working behind the scenes, adding to their ancestral land holdings and consolidating their power base. The imperial title became hereditary in the Habsburg family and, by a calculated policy of dynastic marriages, they enlarged their borders. After centuries of decline, the last vestiges of the Roman Empire in the East finally fell to the Ottoman Turks, leaving this 'leg' of the Empire to pursue its own course. In the West, the greatest of all the Habsburgs, the Emperor Charles V, built a global empire stretching from Vienna to Peru (through the acquisition of the Spanish dominions) and pursued tirelessly the ideal of a unified Christian Empire. He achieved the world's first truly great modern empire, only to be thwarted by the Italian Renaissance spirit with its questioning and criticism of time-honoured institutions, including the Church. This great awakening of learning and knowledge spread north-wards to the German universities, and reached an insignificant monk and educator named Martin Luther. His disgust with the corruption in the Roman Church and Papal abuse of power led to the Protestant Reformation, which spread like wildfire over the Continent. Despite the Emperor's efforts to declare war on the protesters, the old order had been demolished and hopes of religious unity destroyed, along with the meaning of the office of Holy Roman Emperor. He was now the head of just one party – the Catholics. Charles had been crowned Holy Roman Emperor by Pope Clement VII in 1530, the last time the office was bestowed by a Pope. He was the last universal

Emperor of the West, bequeathing a fragmented Empire of political rivalries and religious factions to his diverse successors. There followed 30 years of war, Catholic and Protestant conflagrations, French domination under Louis XIV, the rise of Prussia, the French Revolution, and the emergence of a new star in a firmament of bloodshed, hysteria and domestic turmoil – Napoleon Bonaparte.

Napoleon, too, dreamed of a resurrected Roman-European civilisation, dominated by France. He considered himself the heir and successor to Caesar and Charlemagne and, borrowing a title from ancient Rome, called himself First Consul. With a bust of Julius Caesar adorning his study, classical imagery dominated his mind. 'I am of the race of the Caesars, and of the best, of those who laid the foundations,' he declared. Being completely aware of the influence of the Papacy, he concluded a concordat (an agreement between a pope and a secular government) in 1801, and restored its official status in France. In 1804, he summoned Pope Pius VII to give the highest religious significance to the anointing and crowning of the first Emperor of the French. What followed, a thousand years after the Pope Leo III crowned Charlemagne in Rome, has become one of the most symbolic acts in European history.

As the Pope waited with his cardinals on the high altar of Notre Dame Cathedral, Napoleon approached. All expected him to kneel before the Pontiff and, like Charlemagne, accept a blessing from the superior party. To the amazement of the congregation, he seized the crown from the Pope's hands, turned his back on the Pope and the altar, and crowned himself. In so doing, Napoleon had made it clear that the Church was in the hands of the State, though the coronation went on to be consecrated by the Pope. Napoleon crowned himself again with the 'iron crown' of Lombardy, the great historic symbol of Europe which had previously been worn by Charlemagne, Otto the Great and other European sovereigns. He made himself king of Italy, and sealed a victory over the Russian and Austrian armies. This gave him the confidence to write to Rome:

> 'Tell the Pope I am Charlemagne, the Sword of the Church, his Emperor, and as such I expect to be treated.'

With renewed vigour, he pushed ahead with his plans for a United States of Europe – a league of European states under French hegemony. It soon became clear that the existence of an Austrian archduke with the title Holy Roman Emperor was preposterous. In 1806, Francis II resigned his titles and imperial crown leaving Napoleon as the unchallenged Emperor of the West. But Napoleon's demise was rapid. With a catastrophic attempt to annexe Russia into his empire, and the restoration of the Bourbon king, Louis XVIII, he was defeated by the British at Waterloo and finally exiled to the island of Saint Helena, where he wrote:

> 'I wanted to found a European system, a European code of laws, a European judiciary. There would have been but one people throughout Europe.'

Through further titanic clashes of ambitions, particularly between a second French Empire and a unified German nation, a new German Empire emerged in 1871 – the Second Reich. Simultaneously, a united Italian kingdom emerged and, for the first time in 1500 years, Rome became its capital. Pope Pius IX, stripped of temporal power, began to re-assert his strength in the spiritual realm by declaring Papal Infallibility as a formal article of Catholic belief. Bismarck observed:

> 'What is here at stake is a struggle for power, a struggle as old as the human race, the struggle for power

between monarchy and priesthood. That is a struggle
for power which has filled the whole of German
history.'

In 1882, the ancient links between Italy and Germany were
reforged. This was the prelude to an era which was to arise
more than half a century later, under Adolf Hitler and
Benito Mussolini.

The First World War was a result of Germany's aggres-
sively independent course in foreign affairs, which created a
complex web of alliances. It left more than 10 million people
dead, and a vanquished German Empire. At last, Europe
had fought 'the war to end all wars'. It was, however, only a
matter of time before the harsh terms of surrender imposed
on Germany began to cause severe political, economic and
social problems. Similar conditions prevailed in Italy, with a
disgruntled society plagued by unemployment, strikes and
riots. Through this, Mussolini was handed full emergency
powers, and transformed his government into a fascist
dictatorship. He endeavoured to make Rome once again
the centre of Western civilisation, perceiving himself as a
modern-day Caesar. He even abolished the handshake, re-
instituting instead the old Roman salute with raised arm as
a theatrical gesture towards his dreams of Roman grandeur.

Since Italians are overwhelmingly Roman Catholic,
something had to be done towards settling the Papal
question. Negotiations led to the restoration of the Pope's
temporal power over Vatican City – which became the
smallest sovereign country in the world – and Catholicism
became the official religion of Italy. The rapid rise of
Mussolini was a strong influence on the young Hitler.
Political pandemonium in Germany forged the path for
the emergence of a deliverer, and the Nazis became the
largest party in parliament. So began the development of
the Third Reich. Like Mussolini, Hitler was a Roman
Catholic by birth, and needed to come to terms with the

Vatican. He did so in 1933, in a concordat which gave his government an outward semblance of legitimacy, though relations were strained. In 1936, Mussolini declared the resurrection of the Roman Empire, claiming succession to imperial Rome. He turned to Hitler as an ally, agreeing to co-ordinate foreign policies in the so-called Pact of Steel. The Second World War was to be the means by which Hitler would achieve his mission to become ruler of a great Germanic Empire. It would be a Reich that would rule all of Europe, but his Empire was to be ephemeral. He repeated Napoleon's disastrous mistake of invading Russia, and the tide began to turn. With the suicide of Hitler and the execution of Mussolini, the bloodiest war in history came to an end. It left a ruined Germany once again, a devastated Italy, and a Europe which prayed it had seen the last of its Empire builders.

## The pursuit of Christendom

All these successors of the Roman Caesars understood the vast importance of the Papacy in European affairs. Even at the close of the 20th century, we witness Europe's leaders and the Roman Catholic Church still working together towards the common goal of unity. Many of Europe's political leaders, including Commissioners and MEPs, see a crucial role for the Roman Catholic Church in their efforts, providing a powerfully cohesive common religion to hold Europe together politically. The vision of a Holy Roman Empire under a Roman Catholic aegis is a favourite theme of the present Pope, John Paul II. Indeed, he believes it is his literal calling from God to preside over these crucial immediate years in order to witness it. In Poland, in 1979, he declared:

'Europe, despite its present and long-lasting divisions of regimes, ideologies and economic systems, cannot cease to seek its fundamental unity and must turn to Christianity. Economic and political reasons cannot do it. We must go deeper.'

He went further in 1982, in a speech in Spain, proclaiming:

'I, Bishop of Rome and Shepherd of the Universal Church, from Santiago, utter to you, Europe of the ages, a cry full of love. Find yourself again. Be yourself. Discover your origins, revive your roots.'

The Pope has repeatedly stressed that Europe must seek religious unity if it is to advance beyond political division, and he has prayed for 'all the Christians of East and West, that they become united in Christ and expand the Kingdom of Christ throughout the world.'

According to Malachi Martin, a former Jesuit priest who was at the heart of the Vatican, there is no doubt that John Paul II claims the right to lead the emerging system. Martin's book *The Keys of this Blood*, published in 1990, has the subtitle *Pope John Paul II versus Russia and the West for control of the New World Order*. With its embassies, emissaries, institutions and networks around the world, the Vatican is in a remarkably powerful position to influence global affairs. Martin states:

'What captures the unwavering attention of the secular leaders of the world in this remarkable network of the Roman Catholic Church is precisely the fact that it places at the personal disposal of the Pope a supra-national, supra-continental, supra-trade-bloc structure that is so built and orientated that if tomorrow or next week, by a sudden miracle, a one-world government were established, the Roman Church would not have to undergo any essential change in order to retain its dominant position to further its global aims.'

In the knowledge of this, it is noteworthy that the Vatican has a special status at the United Nations and is able to use its influence in that sphere. The Pope has a privileged right to address the UN General Assembly, while the Holy See has full rights to participate in and speak at UN meetings. No other religious body, Christian or otherwise, is in such a position.

Since World War II, each Pope has thrown his weight behind moves toward the creation of a supra-national European union. Pope John XXIII insisted that Roman Catholics should be 'in the front ranks' of the unification effort. In 1963, Pope Paul VI declared:

> 'Everyone knows the tragic history of our century. If there is a means of preventing this from happening again, it is the construction of a peaceful, organic, united Europe.'

In 1965, he further observed:

> 'A long, arduous path lies ahead. However, the Holy See hopes to see the day born when a new Europe will arise, rich with the fullness of its traditions.'

Perhaps the most concerning of Paul VI's pronouncements on European unification came in Rome, in 1975, when he declared:

> 'Can it not be said that it is faith, the Christian faith, *the Catholic faith that made Europe?'*

He continued:

> 'It is there that *our mission* as bishops in Europe takes on a gripping perspective. *No other human force in Europe can render the service* that is confided to us,

promoters of the faith, to re-awaken Europe's Christian soul, where its unity is rooted.'

Europe was consecrated to Mary by the Vatican in 1309, and placed under her patronage. The shrine of 'Our Lady of Europa', in Gibraltar, was instituted at the consecration. This shrine is being renovated with a £200,000 grant from the EU, about which the Vatican announced:

'It is the prayer of His Holiness that the shrine will be an evermore effective centre of unification, a place where, under the patronage of Mary, the human family will be drawn evermore closely into a fraternal unity and peaceful co-existence.'

The Pope's calls for spiritual unity are echoed by leading politicians all over Europe, especially those allied to the Vatican's political wing, the so-called Christian Democratic parties. One of the most prominent Roman Catholic MEPs is Dr Otto von Habsburg, the eldest son of the last Austro-Hungarian Emperor. Acutely aware of a war-torn Europe, he has long awaited the emergence of a new order. For any future united Europe, he advocates a strong religious role for the Roman Catholic Church, which he terms 'Europe's ultimate bulwark'. He also sees a potential role for the crown of the Holy Roman Empire, which today resides in the Art History Museum of Vienna. Christopher Hollis, in his foreword to Dr Habsburg's book *The Social Order of Tomorrow*, states that Dr Habsburg would like to see Europe resume her essential unity. He writes:

'In the symbolism of that unity, he thinks that the imperial crown of Charlemagne and of the Holy Roman Empire might well have its part to play.'[2]

Habsburg's plea is for a federal Europe so that 'her future can be greater than her past'. A new order of government would thus be crucial.

## Divine rights and wrongs

Just as crucial to the federalising process is the erosion of the achievements of the Reformation. Even some prominent Evangelical Christian leaders have presented this momentous move of God as one of the greatest tragedies that ever happened to the Church, and state that Protestants 'destroyed the unity of Christendom'.[3] They fail to mention the true nature of the Papal system of religion, the depths of spiritual darkness in which it keeps its followers, and its diametric opposition to true biblical Christianity. Unity, it seems, is more important than truth. The concept of Christendom, however unbiblical its practice, appears to matter more than the national boundaries set between one principality and another, regardless of the liberties those boundaries defend.

While visiting Austria in 1983, the Pope spoke out against the 'national and artificial borders' all over Europe. He added:

> 'Europeans should overcome the menacing international confrontations of states and alliances, and create a new united Europe from the Atlantic to the Urals.'

In 1988, he continued this theme when he addressed the European Parliament in Strasbourg; an occasion at which many asked why a perceived spiritual leader was addressing the issues of *political* unity. The *Sunday Telegraph*, in 1991, summed up the Pope's plans for the 'evangelisation' of Europe. It stated:

> 'He is calmly preparing to assume the mantle which he solemnly believes to be his Divine Right – that of new Holy Roman Emperor, reigning from the Urals to the Atlantic.'[4]

It must be noted here that the term 'evangelisation' is a euphemism for the advancement of the social policy and other aims of the Vatican, rather than the proclamation of the Gospel. Among European leaders who have been influential in furthering this social agenda are former Dutch prime minister, Ruud Lubbers, and the former president of the European Commission, Jacques Delors – both Jesuit educated. Chancellor Kohl of Germany and former Spanish prime minister, Felipe Gonzales, are also devout Roman Catholics. For them, there is no nobler task than the unifying of the European continent. A German colleague of Jacques Delors described the idea of a united Europe as 'essentially a Catholic concept',[5] of which an inevitable result would be the subjugation of Britain's Protestant ethos to Roman Catholic social, political and religious teachings. 'The Catholic Churches in many continental countries are influenced by a desire to see a shadow Holy Roman Empire recreated in Europe'[6] and the Christian Democrat and Christian Socialist traditions in Europe are working to that end, bowing to whichever golden calves they have to on the way.

## German 'destiny' – the Fourth Reich

The Christian Democratic Party has held power in Germany since the end of the Second World War. It is strongly influenced by Roman Catholic social teaching, which originated the concepts of solidarity, the single market and the social chapter. These same ideas were expressed by the Nazi Professor Funke, the architect of Hitler's 'New Europe'. In 1942, he issued a compendium of papers which contained chapters and sections on 'The Common European Currency', 'Harmonisation of European Rates of Exchange', 'The European Economic Community', 'The European Agricultural Economic Order' (i.e. The Common Agricultural Policy), 'A Common Labour Policy' and 'The European regional principle' (i.e. The Europe of regions policy). In a summary of collectivist ideas and economic structures, he wrote:

> 'The individual will be replaced by the people, the world market will be replaced by the living space, and capital will be replaced by the organisation of labour.'[7]

These objectives are intrinsic to Roman Catholic social ideals. Rome's motto, *Semper Eadem* (always the same), can certainly be applied to both its desire to direct social thinking and its self-perceived divine mission to preside over a unified Europe, achievable through a dominating German state. Chancellor Kohl has for many years declared his dissatisfaction with a common market of independent states, and believes it is German destiny not merely to lead a European union, but to dominate it. He said:

> 'The *European Union Treaty* introduces a new and decisive stage in the process of European Union, which within a few years will lead to the creation of ... the United States of Europe. There is no alternative to a policy which aims at combination, unless we wish to challenge fate. It has been my policy from the outset to combine indivisibly German unity and the political unification of Europe. For myself, these are two sides of the same coin. We shall only be able to create this greater Europe provided we irreversibly advance the present European core. Both must continue and remain at the top of the agenda: the European Union and the

greater European edifice. There is no question of "either/or" here, but only "both/and".'[8]

In stating this, Chancellor Kohl is merely following his predecessors. The former chancellor of Germany (1950–66) and privy chamberlain to the Pope, Konrad Adenauer, once declared: 'Germany has a divine mission to save Western Europe.' Since the era of Charlemagne, the notion of a German destiny or fate has been deeply engrained in the German psyche; it is an instinct which has driven Germany in the past, and one to which Hitler frequently referred in his speeches. Chancellor Kohl has dominance and destiny at the forefront of his thinking. He has stated:

'The future will belong to the Germans ... when we build the house of Europe ... In the next two years we will make the process of European integration irreversible. This is a really big battle, but it is worth the fight.'

And in Germany there are no means of expressing disapproval of the European dream, since the leader of the opposition party, Oskar Lafontaine, also asserts:

'The United States of Europe has been the aim of the Social Democratic Party all the time.'

At the Tory Party Conference in 1994, a German Christian Democratic Party document was produced. It outlined the CDU's vision for a federal Europe, with a parliament which they stated would be a 'genuine law-making body'. It further stated:

'No country should be allowed to block by veto the efforts of the other countries to deepen integration.'

There can be no other interpretation of these aspirations than that they look to the emergence of a single state, with law-making and tax-raising powers, and that any attempt by a member country to secede would be resisted with force. The CDU document goes on to say:

> 'Never again must there be a destabilizing vacuum of power in central Europe. If European integration were not to progress, Germany might be called upon, or tempted by its own security constraints, to try to effect the stabilization (a word replete with unpleasant historical echoes) on its own, *and in the traditional way.*' [9]

Chancellor Kohl has asserted his conviction that if there were no further European integration, there may well be war. Such alarmist talk from a statesman and politician of his stature is incomprehensible, until it is placed in the context of Germany's conviction about herself and her role in Europe.

Germany's experience as a nation state has been an unhappy one. From Prussian-dominated authoritarianism via the chaos of Weimar leading to Nazi barbarism, her ruling powers have instigated revolution, hyper-inflation, mass unemployment and deliberate wars of attrition. The republic's most recent 50 year period of stability, prosperity and respectability is perceived by many commentators as an historical aberration. They see Germany's potential to revert to type, unless she commits herself to the constraints of the European Union's policy of federal fusion. Most nations were justifiably uneasy about this report, and some were aghast that Germany should insist on such a course.

The Christian Democratic leaders from Belgium, Germany, Greece, Italy, Luxembourg and the Netherlands have all backed far-reaching plans for the transfer of national sovereignty and the establishment of a federal government, with sole control over monetary, foreign and defence policy. [10] From a British perspective, it is not immediately obvious why Germany should want to compromise her sovereignty at all, until one considers the constraints placed on her by the Allies following two world wars. German re-armament could only take place within the context of the North Atlantic Treaty Organisation (NATO). Denied a nuclear capacity of her own, joining organisations which did possess it was clearly an advantageous move. The European People's Party has confirmed its intention 'to set in place by the end of the century a Union with all the necessary political and diplomatic powers ... including a nuclear element.' [11] Whereas the other Western European countries agreed military co-operation through NATO and gave up a measure of independence through their membership of the EEC, these were the organisations through which Germany regained much of her influence. Thus through this process, the German Foreign Minister, Hans-Dietrich Genscher, was able to claim:

'The more European our foreign policy is, the more national it is.' [12]

For Germans, 'pooling sovereignty' has been a means of increasing their national sovereignty. It is, therefore, hard for them to understand the reticence in other member states towards furthering the process of integration.

It is this strong sense of German destiny, and the belief that an attack on Community policy is an attack on German policy, which have led to Chancellor Kohl's threats of war. Karl Lamers, the author of the 1994 CDU paper, asserted: 'The highest interests of the Europeans are identical.' He has since, however, also stated: 'We must control without others noticing.' Germany knows that an increase in European defence will increase her own predominance as the nodal point which links the United States with Russia, and such a strategic positioning would be a fulfilment of her desire to be raised to superpower status, as the head of a united Europe. Controlling the European money supply will be the principal means of gaining supreme power, as the German ambassador to the UK, Dr Jurgen Oesterholt, confirmed in a speech on 12th June 1996:

> 'Germany is unconcerned with the economic experts who are ranged against monetary union. They will be proved irrelevant by the force of European will. It is Germany's historic mission and role to provide that will.' [13]

## The inspirational Euro-vision

There is no doubt that the vision of a united Europe has inspired and continues to inspire politicians, popes and peacemakers of all backgrounds and persuasions. Since a mere free-trade area has failed to inspire anyone, the drive is once again towards a community of nations which will win the hearts and minds of the people, with talk of increased prosperity, dynamic success, secure peace and greater social justice. Many sincere believers quote: *'Where there is no vision, the people perish'* (*Proverbs 29:18*), utterly convinced that a united Europe is God's way forward. At the other extreme are those who would condemn the whole notion of European co-operation as a second Tower of Babel. They see it as being utterly wrong to bring those who speak different languages together under one government – although they conveniently ignore the foundation of the United Kingdom and the British Empire. They also extract a divine charter for the nation state from *Acts 17:26*:

> *'And* (he) *hath made of one blood all nations of men for to dwell on all the face of the earth, and hath determined the times before appointed, and the bounds of their habitation,'*

again conveniently ignoring Paul's concluding explanation: *'That they should seek the Lord.'* The boundaries of the nations can be either an assistance or a hindrance in seeking God. The principal reason the Gospel was able to spread so quickly during the first century was the fact that nations had been unified under Roman rule. The passport of Roman citizenship enabled Paul to travel throughout the Empire unhindered by borders. Time and time again, Scripture is clear on the sovereignty of God:

> *'...the Most High ruleth in the kingdom of men, and giveth it to whomsoever he will.'*          (*Daniel 4:25*)

> *'It is he ... that bringeth the princes to nothing; he maketh the judges of the earth as vanity.'*
>
>                                                            (*Isaiah 40:23*)

> *'He increaseth the nations and destroyeth them: he enlargeth the nations and straighteneth them again.'*
>
>                                                            (*Job 12:23*)

No man-made Euro-vision will succeed against the Lord. The prophet Jeremiah foresaw this tendency in the heart of man:

> *'They speak a vision of their own heart, and not out of the mouth of the Lord.'*          (*Jeremiah 23:16*)

And even within the divine scheme of things, momentous principalities and powers will be warring for control. The fallen state of human nature will be evidenced in corruption in high places, rebellion in low places, hatred, suspicion, jealousy and greed. While sincere democrats will be working to make the Union more stable, democratic and account-able, the opposing forces will be working to make the Union ungovernable. And for those who believe that the divine plan is that Britain should withdraw, or at least that the Government should consult the people in a referendum, then Scripture is equally clear that God raises up new leaders or government ministers to instigate such paths:

> *'... and who knoweth whether thou art come to the kingdom for such a time as this?'*     (*Esther 4:14*)

## References

1. *Treaty of Rome*, Articles 164–188.
2. *The Social Order of Tomorrow*, Otto von Habsburg, Oswald Wolff Publishers, London.
3. *Pro-Europe?*, Sir Fred Catherwood, published 1991, IVP.
4. *Sunday Telegraph*, 21st July 1991.
5. *Financial Times*, 22nd May 1995.
6. *The Rotten Heart of Europe*, Bernard Connolly, Faber & Faber, 1995.
7. 'Europaische Wirtschaftsgemeinschaft', Walter Funke, published 1942, Haude & Spenersche Verlagsbuchhandlung Max Paschke. Quoted from *International Currency Review*, Vol. 23, No. 4, Autumn 1996.
8. *Treason at Maastricht*, Atkinson & McWhirter, 1992.
9. *The Bournemouth Speeches*, Bill Cash MP, Sir James Goldsmith MEP, Rt Hon Lord Tebbit, 1994, The European Foundation.
10. *Daily Telegraph*, 18th February 1992 & *The European*, November 1990.
11. *A secure and peaceful Europe – Europe 2000*, The EPP Action Programme 1994–1999, Brussels, 8th–10th December 1993.
12. *A Response to Chancellor Kohl – A European Germany or a German Europe?*, Bill Cash MP & Iain Duncan-Smith MP, The European Foundation.
13. Speech to the European-Atlantic Group, 12th June 1996.

# Chapter 2

## The Dis-United Kingdom

*'And if a kingdom be divided against itself, that kingdom cannot stand.'*
(*Mark 3:24*)

The current debate about devolution for Scotland, an assembly for Wales and a loosening of ties with Northern Ireland, has encouraged the constituent countries of the United Kingdom to look directly to Brussels as the centre of power and influence, rather than to the British parliament at Westminster. It is natural that these countries begin to see themselves as constituent members of the European Union, independent of United Kingdom government, because the European machine administers their affairs autonomously. Certainly in Scotland, this provides fuel for the nationalist independence cause, and extreme expressions of nationalism can only lead to the total destructuring of the United Kingdom – England for the English, Scotland for the Scots, Wales for the Welsh, and the world already knows of Ireland for the Irish. Yet the Kingdom is not merely made up of four nationalities. Since there is no logical end to regional fracturing, the EU has direct input into numerous 'European Areas', which can only encourage a Yorkshire for the Yorkshiremen, a Cornwall for the Cornish, and so on. Even the Isle of Wight has been prompted into an independence bid as a distinct 'European

Area', and has illegally issued its own currency. Holding the United Kingdom together is a delicate balancing act of political skill and symbolic gestures.

On 3rd July 1996, John Major announced to the House of Commons that the Coronation Stone was to be returned to Scotland. This stone is by tradition Jacob's pillar, mentioned in *Genesis 28:22*, and has come to symbolise nothing less than the anointed foundation of governmental authority. The announcement caused many to focus their attention on the symbolic significance of the stone to the United Kingdom. The return of the Stone of Destiny – otherwise known as the Stone of Scone – to Scotland, after it lay for 700 years in Westminster Abbey as the throne of the United Kingdom, is a significant gesture towards Scottish nationalism. Legend predicts that it heralds the imminent independence of Scotland. After Edward I purloined it for the English in 1296, many Scots saw its position in the Abbey as a sign of Scottish subjugation to Westminster governance, a sign of English oppression and superiority. In reality it has come to symbolise the uniting of the Kingdom under one monarch, who swears to uphold the liberties of all British subjects and govern them according to their customs and laws. Indeed, Queen Elizabeth II has a blood line which is more Scottish than English. In its symbolism, the stone is far more important than the mace in the House of Commons which has to be in place for parliamentary business to proceed. Lying beneath the Coronation Chair in Westminster, it has been the embodiment of the covenant between the Queen-in-Parliament and her subjects, the anointed foundation by which the sovereignty and government of the United Kingdom is upheld. Its removal from the seat of the Queen-in-Parliament leaves a vacuum which will doubtless be filled by the sovereign power of the European Union.

Since the stone's removal was said to have been made with the Queen's approval, a carefully worded statement was issued by the Dean and Chapter of Westminster Abbey. It stated:

> 'The Queen is Visitor of Westminster Abbey and therefore we accept her decision. But, as the successors of those Abbots of Westminster and Deans and Chapters who have been guardians of the stone for so many centuries, we must urge those advising the Queen to take full account of the symbolic and emotional significance of the stone, its integral connection with the Coronation Chair made in 1301 to contain it, and its intimate association with the sacrament of coronation. The stone should not be regarded as a secular museum piece and its religious associations should be respected.'

Many leading scholars of medieval history have challenged the authority of the Prime Minister and the Secretary of State for Scotland, Michael Forsyth, to remove the stone from the Abbey. It has been regarded by many as a low-grade political gimmick. As Dr Christopher Wilson of University College, London, observed:

> 'Edward I may have taken the stone from Scotland, but the important point is that James VI of Scotland, when crowned as James I, adopted the Abbey as the seat of the combined monarchy and had himself buried in the Henry VII chapel, so the new dynasty was well and truly implanted in the Abbey.'

## Mary's dowry and Mary's halo – '12 Forever'

While the political process of European unification undermines the existence of the United Kingdom, the European ecumenical movement is making every effort to remind Christians that the Church is not nationalist, but catholic.

This, of course, is true. The Church meeting in Jerusalem (*Acts 15*) permanently dispelled the notion that the Church is a nationalist pursuit. Christians can and do benefit from an awareness of the wider Church in other cultures the world over. Potentially, though, the word 'catholic' can be misunderstood – rather than taking it to mean 'universal', ecumenical proponents substitute 'Catholic', meaning the Roman Catholic *exclusive* claim to universality. Protestants are perceived by these proponents as being more provincial in their outlook and unwilling to give up their independence or autonomy. Roman Catholicism itself has a strong tendency towards centralism, and views it as wholly necessary for individual nations and churches to merge their individual identities into a larger body, beneath the guise of avoiding future wars and uniting Christian witness. Yet the spiritual values of the Church of Rome, as well as its perceived right to rule in the temporal affairs of the world and its role in global politics, constitute an ethos which is alien to the biblical Protestant traditions of Britain, which are more than 400 years old. Today's climate of compromising ecumenism would have us believe it is possible for the two to co-exist, yet the laws and constitution of the United Kingdom are diametrically opposed by European laws. One has to submit to the other.

In 1953, the Queen swore on oath at her Coronation 'to govern the peoples of the United Kingdom *according to their laws and customs*' and 'to maintain the Protestant Reformed religion established by law.'[1] Both of these are negated by the process of deeper European integration. In a continent in which 61 million claim a Protestant heritage and 199 million profess to be Roman Catholics, it is simply not possible to maintain Protestantism by democratic law. The Protestant constitution of the United Kingdom has long been a strong defence against Rome's desires for the 'evangelisation' of Britain, which the Pope refers to as 'Mary's dowry' – hers by right. The Vatican recognises that

the defeat of Protestantism here would weaken it throughout all Europe, and this has been its aim since the
Reformation. All of the direct military assaults on Britain
from the Spanish Armada to World War II were manifest
failures, but the modern tactics of encirclement and erosion
are bearing fruit.

The *Catholic Herald* recently stated:

> 'The days of the Anglican Church are numbered, and
> most of its worshippers will return to the true faith of
> their distant medieval forebears.'[2]

It is almost a symbolic fulfilment of that prophecy that the
20 pence coin of the British colony Gibraltar, issued by
Parliament and approved by the Queen, bears an engrav-
ing of Mary crowned 'Queen of Heaven' and titled 'Our
Lady of Europa'. The head of the Queen on the other side is
simply titled 'Elizabeth II – Gibraltar', without her usual
titles of D.G. REG. F.D. – Queen by the Grace of God,
Defender of the Faith. As portentous as such obvious
Roman Catholic symbolism is, the British postage stamps
issued in 1984 to commemorate the second election to the
European Parliament went even further. They depicted a
whore riding a beast over seven mounds or waves. Such
imagery has startling similarities to passages from the book
of *Revelation* which a succession of theologians from
Wycliffe to Spurgeon has identified as representing Papal
Rome.

Roman Catholic imagery is endemic in Europe, and has
been wholeheartedly embraced by the European government. The design of the European flag was inspired by the
halo of 12 stars around pictures of the Madonna, and
appears prominently on the Council of Europe stained-glass
window in Strasbourg Cathedral. The window was unveiled
to the world on 11th December 1955, coinciding with the
Roman Catholic feast of the Immaculate Conception.

The Flag Institute (an organisation which provides documentation and research on flags) has examined the evolution of the Council of Europe flag. Its director Dr William Crampton confirms a report that Léon Marchal, the then secretary-general of the Council, said:

> 'It's wonderful that we have got back to the Introit of the new Mass of the Assumption. It's the *corona stellarum duodecim* (the crown of the 12 stars) of the Woman of the Apocalypse.'

Dr Crampton goes on to state:

> 'It was Marchal, the supreme partisan of the Virgin Mary, who suggested the number 12.'

He also mentions a magazine article on the flag's design, which confirmed:

> 'No-one can deny that under these symbols Catholics recognise the presence of the infinitely merciful Queen of Peace in Christ.'[3]

When the European Union was expanded to 15 nations, *The European* Newspaper ran an article[4] responding to those who had expected the flag's design to incorporate 15 stars – one star for each state – similar to the flag of the United States of America. It was confirmed that the 12 gold stars on a blue background were inspired by a picture of 'Our Lady' in Strasbourg, and that they were constant as they were drawn from the 12th chapter of the book of *Revelation*. In the EU's own publication *Europe's Star Choice*, the flag's inspiration is explained under the chapter heading '12 Forever'. It is also stated that Strasbourg is a city which symbolises the dream of Franco-German integration – the heart of the Empire of Charlemagne.

Significantly, when the booklet goes on to describe the flags of all the member states, the flag of the United Kingdom is the only one to be criticised. The booklet's authors state that it is 'a disgrace' that Wales is not represented. While the criticism may be valid, the vehemence of the objection is noticeable.

It is also concerning, though some may dismiss it as trivially amusing, that a Roman Catholic Englishman[5] sent a letter to Jacques Delors, with the suggestion of dedicating the European Union to the 'Blessed Virgin Mary'. He had presumably noted that Delors had been responsible for promoting the European flag, with its unmistakable Marian symbolism showing a circle of 12 stars on a blue background. The member of Delors's private office responsible for the Commission President's relations with the Catholic Church replied that the suggestion was gratefully received, but that the President did not feel that it was within his authority to respond affirmatively. Was this because such a decision had to be placed before the European Council, or the Parliament, or even before the peoples of Europe in a referendum? Sadly, no. Elucidation came as the President stated that he would make the suggestion known to the Holy Father. If, 'after prayerful consideration', the Holy Father considered it appropriate, Delors would do everything he could to implement it. Is this an indication of the real spiritual authorities ruling Europe? Thankfully, since nothing more was heard, presumably the Pope didn't much like the idea.

## A Roman Catholic Church of England?

Clifford Longley, a former religious affairs correspondent of *The Times*, gave an address to the Roman Catholic Bishops' Conference in 1993 setting out a strategy for the Roman Catholic Church in this country to become the leading church. In the address, entitled 'Becoming a

National Church', he traced the growth of the Anglo-Catholic movement within the Church of England. He concluded that the conversion of England would be accomplished as the movement permeated the Anglican tradition, rather than through individual conversions. There have been several recent turmoils within the Church of England, such as the ordination of women priests, the re-defining of co-habitation before marriage as no longer 'living in sin', the announcement by the former Archbishop of Canterbury, Lord Runcie, that he knowingly ordained practising homosexual clergy, and the recent high profile conversions to Rome of prominent members of Parliament and members of the Royal Family. All of these constitute an unprecedented disintegration of an institution which has shaped our heritage, forged our freedom and established biblical Christian principles at the core of British government and society. In an age where all the old institutions – Monarchy, Parliament and Church – are being discredited and marginalised, the Roman Catholic Church is being given an open invitation to fill the vacuum created and set a moral agenda to stabilise an uncertain society. It will be perceived as an unchanging bedrock upon which a new order may be constructed. Its plea will be for Britain, as for Europe, to seek out its lost soul and restore its 'Christian' spirituality. The more the Church of England is perceived as a failure, the greater the opportunity will be for the Church of Rome to proceed with its 'evangelisation' and absorb Britain into a Catholic Europe.

Relations between the Vatican and Britain have become increasingly closer in recent decades. Since the Second World War, the British Government has recognised the temporal authority claimed by the Pope. Also, since 1980, the Royal Court of St. James has had a Papal Nuncio (a Vatican ambassador to a foreign court). Relations were improved further when the Queen visited the Pope at the Vatican and willingly wore black in order to be received by him. Perceived by successive popes as a heretic, the Queen would not have been granted an audience unless she had symbolically submitted herself to the radiance of his whiteness. This she did, to the dismay of many Christians back home, and to the insult of those Protestant martyrs who died during the reigns of her forebears. This rapprochement reached its culmination when Pope John Paul II visited Britain in 1982, the first Pope to do so since the Reformation. He held joint services with the Archbishop of Canterbury and was received by the Queen. Since then, there have been further meetings between the Pope and prominent members of the Royal Family, and also between the Pope and the present Archbishop of Canterbury, Dr George Carey. In former times, such a series of happenings would have been unthinkable.

After the Reformation and the adoption of the 39 Articles of the Church of England, the Church and State laid their foundations upon the authority of the Bible and a Protestant monarchy. However, the present Queen, in 1996, appointed an influential Roman Catholic as her chaplain, and attended Vespers in Westminster Cathedral to celebrate the centenary of the building as Britain's Roman Catholic centre. Further, Prince Charles, the Heir to the Throne, is professing an allegiance not to biblical Christianity but to all faiths. The Coronation Oath is clearly being ignored and undermined through these changes, in a prelude to the removal of the *Act of Settlement* of 1701, which does not permit a Roman Catholic, or a monarch married to a Roman Catholic, to accede to the throne. If this happened, for the first time since the Glorious Revolution of 1688, Rome would be provided with a vassal monarch with sovereignty over 'Mary's dowry'. This would inevitably lead to the ascendancy of Roman traditions over the authority of Scripture which lies at the heart of Protestantism and the institution of the Monarchy.

An illustration of the Queen's vassal status has been

highlighted by one Church of England vicar. He enquired of his diocese registrar (being responsible for legal matters) whether his Oath of Allegiance to the Queen effectively means he has sworn allegiance to Brussels. He suggested that because the Queen's sovereignty had been removed, through her imposed European citizenship and her account-ability to the European Courts, his loyalties were now to the greater sovereign power. The question was put to Bucking-ham Palace, who did not immediately know the answer. They in turn consulted Brussels on the matter – a simple act which clearly displayed the Queen's subjection to a govern-ing power other than Westminster. Since Buckingham Palace chose not to consult any of Her Majesty's ministers of state, her vassalhood has been established.

In 1993, the first sacrament of penance or 'confession' since the Reformation was held at the Palace of West-minster. This was followed by a High Mass to celebrate the reception of a junior social security minister into the Roman Church from the Church of England. Such events fly in the face of the Queen's promise 'to maintain to the utmost of (her) power the Laws of God, *the true profession of the Gospel* and the Protestant Reformed religion established by law', and her added assurance, with Bible in hand:

> 'The things I have here before promised *I will perform and keep*. So help me God.'

In swearing this, she committed herself *and the Crown-in-Parliament* to uphold the supremacy of Scripture. Every Member of Parliament swearing their Oath of Allegiance to the Queen, while not being constrained in their individual conscience to profess the Christian faith, is certainly declar-ing their commitment to defend biblical Christianity. Allegiance to the Queen must, at the very least, demand a defence of her oaths and promises to her subjects.

Unlike other European nations with monarchies, the British throne is not merely a symbol of popularity or an ingredient of constitutional ceremony with minor political functions, but the maintaining legal foundation of biblical Christianity on these shores. It is not therefore appropriate to compare defence of the British throne with other European monarchies. The Danes, the Dutch, the Belgians and the Spanish do not have constitutions which prevent the ascendancy of a Roman Catholic monarch, leading to submission to Rome. The prospect of the removal of the *Act of Settlement* from the Statute Books, a change which the Queen and other senior members of the Royal Family are reported to favour, would be the crowning glory of the Anglo-Roman Catholic International Commission. The signs are already evident. On the significance of Prince Charles' bedside rosary, a gift from the Pope, The *Sunday Telegraph* reported:

> 'How changed is our country. Even 30 years ago, the news that the future Supreme Governor of the Church of England practised what would have been considered a Popish superstition would have provoked outrage. A century before it might have provoked revolution. The news about a mistress would have attracted far less attention.'

As Scripture warns:

> *'If the foundations be destroyed, what can the righteous do?'* (*Psalm 11:3*)

Journalists may speculate on the precise function and role of the monarchy, but they ignore the fact that its crucial raison d'être is to uphold the Protestant Reformed Religion, established by law, and to maintain the laws of God and the profession of the true Gospel. The *Coronation Oath Act* and the *Act of Settlement* could not be clearer, yet the removal of either Act would leave the monarchy with no clear reason for existing. The Church of Rome knows this. Such an undermining of the British throne would be a mortal blow, and would endanger its very existence. From the Protestant throne came Britain's religious and civil liberties, and their continuing existence would inevitably also be endangered.

## References

1.  *Coronation Oath Act*, 1953, Section IV.
2.  *Catholic Herald*, December 1993.
3.  *Médiatrice et Reine*, 1973.
4.  *The European*, 14th–20th December 1995.
5.  He is unnamed in *The Rotten Heart of Europe*, Bernard Connolly, Faber & Faber, 1995.

# Chapter 3

## Sovereignty

*'Your sovereignty has been removed.'*
*(Daniel 4:31* NASB)

The judgement of God upon King Nebuchadnezzar is a
constant reminder that the kingdoms of the earth belong to
the Lord. They are his to give, and his to take away.
Throughout the entire history of Israel, God has judged its
rebellion and idolatry by permitting numerous invasions by
foreign powers:

> *'And now I have given all these lands into the hand of*
> *Nebuchadnezzar the king of Babylon.'* *(Jeremiah 27:6)*

His sovereignty was in turn removed by the Medes and the
Persians, who were themselves succeeded by the Greeks and
then by the Romans. Sovereignty has a clear scriptural
significance. Although the loss of it may not necessarily be a
bad thing – for example in co-operating on matters of the
environment, drug-trafficking or terrorism – it is clearly
wrong when it is lost through deception and manipulation.
Under such circumstances, the ordinary people have the
right to know precisely what is at stake. The former Speaker
of the House of Commons, Lord Tonypandy, wrote to *The*
*Times* on 24th April 1995:

'The current slide towards a single European currency threatens both our economic and political independence, and thus our sovereignty. Subterfuge and half-truths have been used to persuade the nation that neither our sovereignty nor our relationship with the Commonwealth is endangered ... For more than 600 years Speakers of the House of Commons have fiercely defended the supremacy of the Westminster Parliament. As one whose privilege it was to follow humbly in the steps of the past, I call upon our nation to awake, and to demand that the voice of the people shall be heard before the next intergovernmental conference takes irrevocable decisions affecting our sovereignty. A referendum conducted before, and not after, further decisions are taken is our elementary right. This is the only sure way to prevent our parliamentary sovereignty, our judicial system, and our Commonwealth relationships from being grievously undermined.'

There is much debate over precisely what is meant by an 'independent sovereign state'. A nation is independent when it is self-governing. Those nations which are self-governing and operating a multi-party parliamentary democracy can be described as being independent, and their citizens are free. To these states, the adjective 'sovereign' can be applied. One of the guiding principles of the Constitution of the United States of America was the 'sovereignty of the people' – the notion of sovereignty as the inalienable possession of the individual. Sovereignty flows upwards from the individual to various layers of government, and is indissociable from democracy, since the only way for the individual to exercise his sovereignty is through democracy. Intrinsic to this is the notion that what the individual can grant through the ballot box, he can also take away. While sovereignty may be temporarily exercised by a parliament, it never becomes an exclusive possession of the governmental institutions. The power to revoke, renounce or renegotiate treaties freely entered into is part of what defines an independent sovereign state, and this freedom can never be limited irrevocably. It should be held and exercised in trust on behalf of the individuals who collectively make up the people, and handed back to them intact after the prescribed parliamentary period of government. It is this notion of sovereignty that sits best with British traditions and instincts.

With sovereignty defined, it is evident that Britain is no longer an independent sovereign state, by virtue of her membership of the EU. In ever-increasing areas of national life, no vote of MPs in the House of Commons, however overwhelming, can affect, change or block decisions taken by EU bodies. Even a landslide vote in a British general election would have minimal impact on decision-making by EU institutions and their implementation in Britain. British electors now have a severely curtailed ability to express their wishes through the ballot box.

This irrevocability[1] and irreversibility[2] of Community law are at the heart of the EU. The concept of *acquis communautaire* is just that – 'what has been acquired cannot be taken away'. The *Maastricht Treaty* specifically prevents any alterations to *acquis communautaire*. The move towards a single currency (i.e. the comprehensive surrender of national economic management to a supra-national body) is irrevocable and irreversible.

The President of the Evangelical Alliance and former prominent MEP, Sir Fred Catherwood, dismisses the whole sovereignty issue as a non-argument in his book *Pro-Europe?*. He sees it as a pretext to indulge in nationalism, a dressed-up means of expressing power. Since his publishers claim the book makes 'a distinctly Christian contribution to this far-reaching debate', it is implied that to disagree with his conclusions invites accusations of holding un-Christian convictions. Nevertheless, Lord Tonypandy is unafraid of clearly stating in his foreword to Sir Fred's book:

> 'I personally do not share all his convictions ... I do not want to see the United Kingdom as one 12th or possibly one 20th of a federal Europe. No former Speaker of the House of Commons could possibly want to see that historic legislative chamber reduced to the equivalent of a county council.'

Sovereignty is neither a mere indulgence nor a pretext, but a very real issue which is right at the root of the question: 'Who governs Britain?'

## A country called 'Europe'?

There is little doubt that extreme expressions of nationalism lead to all manner of undesirable social ills. However, the Europhiles who express an abhorrence of British nationalism are themselves in danger of expressing a Euro-nationalism in their zeal to construct an exclusively European economic, political and military union. Euro-nationalism also demands total allegiance and, like any other nationalism, can become a political religion, compelling adherents to the conclusion that the nation state of Europe is their one and only hope. This can develop easily into a cult. Even those who argue that the nations of Europe are our neighbours and we are commanded to love them seem to blind themselves to the fact that a European Union will itself have borders and our 'new' neighbours will be Africa, Asia and the Middle East – but no-one is proposing we fuse vast continents together in order to openly express any partnership. This Euro-introspection comes from an antipathy towards some 'other', notably America and Japan. Some political scientists see the emerging Europe as a new form of political structure, defined more by its antagonisms to the 'Anglo-Saxon' world and to Japan than by its structures for advancing the interests of member nation states.

> 'Delors wants to create a new state, "Europe", and to create with it a new "nation" based on some supposed cultural identity that can be defined only in terms of what it is not, what it is antithetical to.'[3]

The movement towards a federal Europe is a very real threat, and the danger is not being exaggerated. Of course, the word 'federal' is not actually used in the *Maastricht Treaty*, but its character is evident nonetheless. The document states:

> 'By this Treaty, the High Contracting Parties establish among themselves a European Union.'

Since the word 'union' is defined as a 'joining together; a making into one; a combining or amalgamating', it is clear that a European *State* has been created, and a common European Citizenship established. Consequences of this include Britain's obligation under the treaty to submit its economic plans to Brussels, ensuring proper submission to European governance. Also, the fact that German nationals may now freely vote in British elections, or Italians in French elections, is plainly the course of federalism. British territory and its tiers of government no longer remain independent and autonomous. In May 1996, the European Court of Justice judged that Britain had acted illegally in banning the export of sheep to Spain for slaughter. Despite the film footage of the appallingly illegal methods used in many Spanish abattoirs, including lambs being hung upside down by one leg and their throats being cut while fully conscious, the European Court prevented Britain from taking action to prevent such cruelty. Scripture makes clear:

> *'A righteous man regardeth the life of his beast: but the tender mercies of the wicked are cruel.'*
>
> (*Proverbs 12:10*)

On an occasion when the British Government attempts to enact a righteous law consistent with Scripture, the European Court intervenes.

Territorial autonomy has further been tested by the recent arguments over fishing rights. As the whole world recognises Britain's 200 mile territorial waters, the Common Fisheries Policy rules them to be European waters, holding 60 per cent of the EU's fish stocks, but Britain is only allocated a quota of 30 per cent, reduced further still by the 'quota-hopping' of the Spanish. As Brussels has handed to all European citizens the right to vote, live and work in the UK, visa controls from non-EU countries (e.g. the USA, the Commonwealth and the Middle East) are also soon to be passed to their control.

All this is consistent with the intention to work towards a common foreign policy. The *Maastricht Treaty* further states:

> 'The Union and its Member States shall define and implement a common foreign and security policy.'

Its objectives shall be:

> 'To safeguard the common values, fundamental interests and independence of the European Union.'

Sir Fred Catherwood asserts that this is the 'only' way Europe can avoid conflict because *'voluntary* political co-operation is *not strong enough.'* [4] It seems that the last 50 years of peace have been a distinct failure, and now

Britain needs a 'binding agreement' to ensure its foreign and defence policies are tied to the EU's. The Labour Party is quite prepared to trade Britain's sovereignty for what it terms 'more effective EU decisions', and has stated:

> 'The failed Tory project of confrontation has to be replaced with a culture of co-operation.'

Further, they state:

> 'It might be necessary to trade part of national sovereignty,'

arguing that

> 'losing some of that sovereign power might be in the interests of the people.'[5]

What the Labour Party has failed to understand is that Britain's sovereignty is not *theirs* to trade away – it belongs to the British people. Members of Parliament are meant to be the *guardians* of sovereignty and democracy, not the owners of them, and only by consulting the people can such a vast constitutional shift ever be made acceptable. It is the duty of government ministers to serve the nation whose people elected them to office above all other considerations, and most especially when the very continuation of the nation is at risk. The *Maastricht Treaty* has already taken Britain further down the federal path than politicians ever had the moral right to tread. The 'Europe' of this treaty is clearly defined as a Union which is intended to be more than the sum of its parts – a federal supra-national state – and which leaves the House of Commons increasingly irrelevant as political power gradually transfers to Brussels. Many of Britain's European partners are, of course, wholly committed to such a transfer.

There are those who view a federal Europe as an inevitable part of a glorious New World Order of peace and co-operation. A Congress of Europe, convened at the Hague in 1948, adopted *Seven Resolutions on Political Union* as the way forward. Resolution number seven asserts:

> 'The creation of a United Europe must be regarded as an essential step towards the creation of a United World.'

Sovereignty consequently becomes an outdated concept, and globalists point to many external events and trends which already determine or affect Britain's policies, in particular the British membership of NATO. The important consideration, however, is that no external trends or decisions, and least of all those made by NATO, hinder Britain's capacity for *independent* decision-making. Only by remaining free as a nation can Britain adapt to change, according to her choices and priorities, rather than being obliged to accept the policies and decisions of others. The function of NATO has remained the same since its inception; it permits common policies and voluntary alliances between nations, but does not prevent them from acting unilaterally where the need arises. NATO has involved no erosion of sovereignty, since the British Government surrendered none of its capacity for independent decision-making.

The European fixation with target dates and deadlines creates an immense pressure to establish the European political federation within a fixed time. This is causing a destabilising of Britain, and the whole turbulent and uncertain European project is in danger of impeding the implementation of the globalists' broader plans for the world. The whole agenda has to be kept rigorously on schedule.

# Building on the sands of deceit

Harold Wilson's 1975 Referendum on Britain's continued membership of the EEC assured the British people that sovereignty would not be eroded and, on that understanding, the electorate voted to remain members of the EEC. The assurance given to both the British people and to Parliament in 1973 by the then prime minister, Edward Heath, was that there was 'no question of any erosion of essential national sovereignty.' In other words, Britain was to be part of a community of sovereign nations who wished to trade with each other. Over and over again, that was the message that was hammered home to the electorate. Heath further gave the assurance:

> 'There are some in this country who fear that in going into Europe, we shall in some way sacrifice independence and sovereignty ... These fears, I need hardly say, are completely unjustified ...'

The truth is that much more was surrendered than the electorate was led to believe. The European Court of Justice states:

> 'Every national court must apply Community law in its entirety and must accordingly set aside any provision of national law which may conflict with it, whether prior to or subsequent to the Community rule.'[6]

It is now generally accepted by British judges that European law takes precedence over Acts of Parliament. Parliament has, therefore, surrendered its sovereignty. Where there is any disagreement about Britain's actions, it is the European Court of Justice which decides what is right. The former Master of the Rolls, Lord Denning, stated:

> 'No longer is European law an incoming tide flowing up the estuaries of England. It is now like a tidal wave

bringing down our sea walls and flowing inland over our fields and houses, to the dismay of us all.' [7]

It would be accurate to state that *all* the known facts about the precise nature of the European beast were not clearly revealed to the British people. Even as Heath was assuring Parliament of the sanctity of Britain's sovereignty and the maintenance of her global trading outlook, he was deceiving the people – a deception which has recently been revealed. The Lord Chancellor wrote to Heath on 14th December 1960 in response to Heath's enquiry into the constitutional implications of becoming a signatory to the *Treaty of Rome*. He stated:

'To satisfy the requirements of the treaty, Parliament could enact legislation which would give automatic force of law to any existing or future regulations made by ... the Community. This would go far beyond the most extensive delegation of powers, even in wartime, that we have ever experienced ... It is clear ... that the (European) Council of Ministers could eventually ... make regulations which would be binding on us even against our wishes ... It is the first step on the road which leads ... to the fully federal state.'

As the most senior legal officer in the land, he went on to warn:

'I must emphasise that in my view the surrenders of sovereignty involved are serious ones ... these objections ought to be brought out into the open ...'

To have been warned of this, and then to continue with the assertion that there would be no loss of sovereignty, is blatant proof of Heath's duplicity.

President Georges Pompidou of France provided an interesting degree of illumination on the real facts. He said:

> 'I asked the British Prime Minister what he thought of Europe, in other words, whether Britain was really determined to become European, whether Britain, which is an island, was determined to tie herself to the Continent, and whether she was prepared, consequently, to loosen her ties with the open sea, towards which she had always looked. And I can say that the explanations and views expressed to me by Mr Heath are in keeping with France's concept of the future.'[8]

Further, West Germany's former foreign minister, Walter Scheel, affirmed in 1971: 'The aim remains a European Government.'[9] The federalist goal of the European Community was clearly evident from its beginning and therefore, intentionally or not, the pro-European leaders of 1975 deceived the British electorate. In a BBC interview in 1990, Heath was directly asked whether, when he took Britain into Europe, he really had in mind a United States of Europe with a single currency (i.e. the complete opposite of what the electorate were told by his government). He answered: 'Of course, yes.' This was a breathtaking admission, showing clearly that the Heath government's White Paper and subsequent referendum held in 1975 had been fraudulent. He was not seeking a community of sovereign nations, as his government had promised, but a federal European superstate.

One of the founding fathers of the EU, Jean Monnet, also a devout Roman Catholic, totally rejected the idea that Europe should consist of sovereign nations. He believed in the Catholic vision that Europe should become a federal superstate, into which all ancient nations would be fused. 'Fused' is the word he used in a communication dated 30th April 1952, and is wholly consistent with the language of the *Maastricht Treaty*. For this to be achieved without the peoples of Europe realising what was happening, the plan was to be accomplished in successive steps. Each was to be disguised as having an economic purpose, but all, taken together, would inevitably and irreversibly lead to federation. After Europe's coal and steel production were pooled, Europe's atomic programmes were to be co-ordinated. Then would follow the Common Agricultural Policy and the Common Market. After this would come the single currency, and so on. Monnet related on 6th May 1970, that he had explained this to Heath. He said:

'I told Heath how we had proceeded from the start, step by step, and how in this way we had gradually created the Common Market and today's Europe, and that I was convinced we should proceed in the same manner.'

There may have been no evil intent; Heath and other leaders may have thought that they knew best and that the people should simply follow them, uninformed or, if necessary, disinformed. But the anti-EEC leaflet of the 1975 Referendum plainly set out the dangers of such a federation, warning:

'The fundamental question is whether or not we remain free to rule ourselves in our own way ... the Common Market ... sets out by stages to merge Britain with France, Germany, Italy and other countries into a single nation ... our right, by our votes, to change policies and laws in Britain will steadily dwindle.'

The then leader of the Labour Party, Hugh Gaitskell, uttered the same warning at the 1962 Labour Party Conference, and spoke of 'the end of Britain as an independent nation state ... the end of a thousand years of history. You may say "let it end" but, my goodness, it is a decision that needs a little care and thought.' This may have sounded histrionic at the time, but successive European treaties have shown that his fears clearly had foundation.

God, of course, will speak through whom He wills, whatever the person's faith or belief. The story of Balaam (*Numbers 22–24*) proves that the Lord is prepared to speak truth through a numb-skulled, money-grabbing seer, or even through his ass. Whether Balaam is considered a sinner or saint, a believer in the one true God or not, there is no doubt he was inspired to declare God's will and was given a vision of Israel's future destiny. Similarly, many people who have been considered 'numb-skulls' in their time have sounded warnings about Britain's future destiny, and have been given national platforms from which to do so. The following article from *The Times* of 4th June 1975, written by Enoch Powell, may have been a word of prophecy; it has touches of Jeremiah-like foreboding. Like Jeremiah, Enoch Powell was dismissed by the people as an eccentric merchant of doom. Certainly its accuracy of perception is unquestionable, and his arguments have more relevance today than they had 20 years ago:

'It is the old, old worry: will the British people perceive in time what is happening to them and where they are being taken? If they do, I am not afraid for the outcome. But will they?

'I suppose there is rarely or never an absolute last chance, though the vocabulary of politicians would be seriously impoverished without the phrase; and referendum day is certainly not the last chance, because I am sure that, if the result is interpreted as Stay In, the events of the following months will open many eyes that are closed at present. Perhaps, however, I might express it this way: if referendum day is not September 1939, at any rate it is September 1938.

'The nation is being invited to confirm the surrender, and the permanent surrender, of its most precious possession: its political independence and parliamentary self-government, the right to live under laws and to pay taxes authorised only by Parliament and to be governed by policies for which the executive is fully accountable through Parliament to the electorate. Above and beyond all the arguments about butter mountains and Brussels bureaucrats there lies a stark fact, undenied and undeniable.

'It is undenied because that is what the *European Communities Act* of 1972 says; it is undeniable because that is why the advocates of British membership commend it. The difficulty is that to most British people the thing is inconceivable – as I remember that the idea of the Second World War was inconceivable to most of them during most of the 30s. "But surely," they often say, "the French and the Germans and the other member states have not given up their independence and self-government, and don't intend to." The question – and the answer to it – are typical of the mutual incomprehension between Britain and the Continent in matters political.

'The answer is, "Yes, they have given up their independence and self-government; they fully intended this and that to them is what the EEC is about."

'Let us take a closer look at the founder Six. The West Germans make no secret of not merely not desiring, but actually fearing to be an independent nation: the EEC is for them an insurance against themselves. For the Low Countries – Benelux – national independence was something never more than precariously secured to them by a balance of power in Western Europe in which, with good reason from experience, they have lost faith. Their position as provinces in a West European state, or as states in a West European federation, would represent no noticeable loss. In Belgium especially the pride of independence and distinctiveness and of self-government has belonged, since the Middle Ages, to the city and not to the territory.

'About the strength and reality of the national pride of the French there is no manner of doubt, but it attaches neither to independence nor still less to democratic self-government. The Fifth Republic is nearer to an elective dictatorship than to parliamentary democracy. A Frenchman in the Council of Ministers, or the will of the French executive brought to bear through the institutions of the Community, is for France the reality of national power – the wider stage on which Louis XIV, Bonaparte or General de Gaulle perform the greater glory of France. Nothing could be more remote from French experience or conception than our British inability to understand liberty and nationhood apart from the supremacy and independence of Parliament.

'Italian nationality owes even less to parliamentary self-government than does that of France. A federation of European states in which Italy was absorbed would seem but a natural extension of the process by which modern Italy was so recently assembled from its diverse component parts.

'The case of Italy is a reminder too that all the founder states of the Community, in sharp contrast with ourselves, are historically familiar with the idea of a larger and European imperium exercising an acknowledged, if for long a shadowy, authority which oversteps national boundaries. The rule of an external law is nothing new or strange to them, whereas for close on 500 years – the whole of our history since the Middle Ages – the very notion has been totally repugnant to the English. When kings like Henry VIII, and

Edward I before him, declared that "this realm is an empire of itself", they were speaking the mind of the Englishman.

'Even when the Community seems to our ears to be using the language of parliamentary sovereignty, it is really talking about something quite different. The directly elected European parliament, which is integral to the *Treaty of Rome* and which the other members of the Community are serious in envisaging for no more than two or three years ahead, has nothing but the name in common with what we mean by Parliament and what Parliament means to us. It is another instrument for creating a new artificial state, a delegate assembly perfectly intelligible and familiar to member states whose written constitutions, which brought them into existence, prescribed just such assemblies.

'To us, a parliament not representing an electorate so homogeneous as to accept the majority as binding the minority and the institution as endowing with authority the outcome of debate, is an absurdity or a monstrosity, a device in our terms essentially undemocratic. Parliament for us does not produce unity: it is the expression of a pre-existing unity.

'The British people have no notion of what the rest of the Community assumes that they are meaning by accepting membership. The mutual misunderstanding would only be heightened and rendered more dangerous if British membership appeared to be confirmed by a method which the rest would mistake for the equivalent of one of their own constitutional procedures.

'Before and during the referendum campaign, the supporters of British membership, with a few honourable exceptions, have not only not endeavoured to make this clear to the electors, they have gone out of their way to soothe away any suspicion that the renunciation of nationhood through Community membership is fundamental, deliberate and relatively imminent. All the more bitter and damaging would be the revulsion on both sides when the realisation eventually dawned that each had been deceived. "Albion Perfide" is a slander; but it is a slander we have often courted, and never more recklessly than now.'

When Enoch Powell so directly confronted the lies of the Heath government, he was dismissed by many as a bigoted eccentric, and was marginalised as an irrelevance. As the decades have passed, his words have rung with an alarming truth, but prophets and prophecy are always easier to understand and interpret in retrospect. Whatever the British future may be, it is still God who *'removeth kings and setteth up kings' (Daniel 2:21)*, and many may judge that Britain deserves to have her sovereignty removed and be handed over to the ruling power emerging on the Continent. It may be that only a profound and sincere repentance will halt the process. Society is becoming increasingly godless, and Christian principles count no more highly than humanist philosophy. The battle for the soul of Britain has never been so great, nor so subtle.

## References

1. *Maastricht Treaty*, Article 109 1 4.
2. *Ibid*, Protocol on Transition to Third Stage.
3. *The Rotten Heart of Europe*, Bernard Connolly, Faber & Faber, 1995.
4. *Pro Europe?*, Sir Fred Catherwood, 1991, IVP.
5. *The Guardian*, 14th June 1996.
6. Case 106/77, Amministrazione delle Finanze dello Stato v. Simmenthal, 1978, ECR 629 at 643,644, quoted in *The Times*, 1st April 1996.
7. *The ECJ: Judges or Policy Makers?*, Gavin Smith, quoted in *The Times*, 1st April 1996.
8. *The Truth about a Federal Europe*, The Freedom Association.
9. *Ibid*.

# Chapter 4

# The Oligarchical Democracy

*'There is neither Jew nor Greek, there is neither slave nor free, there is neither male nor female; for you are all one in Christ Jesus.'*                    (*Galatians 3:28*)

Democracy is the form of government in which supreme power is vested in the people collectively, and is administered by them or by officers appointed by them. It was an achievement of the Renaissance and the Reformation that the significance of the individual was brought to the fore. The concept of government by democracy had been inherited from ancient Greece. This philosophy, coupled with the Protestant emphasis on the individual's personal relationship with God, and his right to read and interpret Scripture for himself, heralded the decline of government by autocrats, in either the Church or State. The New Testament teaching that the Church consisted of the 'priesthood of all believers' also encouraged the growth of freedom of conscience. Such liberties gave rise to the realisation of the dignity and responsibility of the individual, and of his ultimate accountability to God, and led to the creation of the earliest democracies. Britain, the United States of America, the Netherlands, Denmark, Norway and Sweden developed first, followed by the British Dominions, Canada, Australia and New Zealand. As each nation became a self-governing democracy, the notion of a distant and over-mighty executive declined.

The 'spirit' of autocracy, however, remains a very real power on the Continent. Its clash with Christianity and liberty is most clearly discernible when one examines the political consequences of the atheistic philosophy of Marx and Nietzsche, and their disciples, Lenin, Mussolini and Hitler. Denying the existence of God, or replacing the God of the Bible with their own idolatrous beliefs, these were the prophets and architects of totalitarianism – a form of government engrained in the psyches of many nations, and which seems to have flared up in each generation since the French Revolution of 1789. Totalitarianism, where everything is brought under the control of one authority and no opposition is allowed, is at the core of Roman Catholicism, and many continental countries are wholly at ease with the essence of government by dictatorship, even if that government calls itself democracy. Otto von Habsburg asserts:

> 'True democracy cannot exist under a regime animated by the ideas of the French Revolution ... A materialistic ideology of this kind ... can rarely go beyond pure power politics.'

And power is precisely what the politics of Europe is about. The *Sunday Telegraph* put its finger on the problem by quoting a report by Marc Luyckx, a full-time EU official. It said:

> 'Catholics tend to be vertical, hierarchical and centralised ... in other words, they tend to be corrupt, autocratic, with more susceptibility to the Mafia and maximum bureaucracy.'

Protestant countries, on the other hand, such as Britain or Denmark, tend to be more democratic and open, with less tolerance of centralised control. This is vital if we are to understand the Danish rejection of the *Maastricht Treaty*. As one commentator observes:

> 'They thought the Community was about trade, something they could understand. Now they feel trapped in a community of Latins and Continentals.'

It is unsurprising, therefore, that the whole European debate has been at its most fierce in those nations whose heritage is Protestant, and not in the slightest bit surprising that continental neighbours simply cannot understand what all the fuss is about.

Consider the case of 'subsidiarity', which European leaders and the British Government have assured the people is a form of decentralisation. Supposedly, it ensures that power is not concentrated in Brussels. It cannot, however, be applied in retrospect to those considerable powers which have already been transferred there. According to the *Maastricht Treaty*, those powers simply cannot be touched; Brussels owns them forever; they are *acquis communautaire*, and therefore sacrosanct. In the EU, movement is only one way: towards federalism, which is why words like 'irreversible' and 'fusion' are so frequently on the lips of Eurocrats. There is no room here for reform. In a true democracy, it is the people who decide which powers to lend to their leaders. In a false democracy, it is the leaders who decide which freedoms to lend to the people.

## The Bible and government

It would be erroneous to conclude that the Bible supports any particular political system above another. It certainly speaks nothing of our modern concept of democracy. However, it is equally true to state that the broad principles of government, law, justice and civil order which gave rise to our democracy were founded on the Judeo-Christian political and social implications of Scripture, and particularly the notion of individual equality before God. Discrimination on the basis of wealth is forbidden (*James 2:1–7*). Jesus was the son of a carpenter, and the apostles who were entrusted with the foundation of the Church were mainly fishermen. Jesus cared for the ordinary man, and readily mixed with groups of people who were considered outcasts. Paul states:

> '*Not many of you were wise by human standards; not many were influential; not many were of noble birth.*'
> (*1 Corinthians 1:26*)

The early Church *was* the individual people, not a building or a hierarchy. There are no references to popes, archbishops or cardinals; just ordinary men and women. The first elders were no more important than their flocks. They were all equal in Paul's eyes because each one mattered to God and was known by name.

If Christianity made it entirely plain that each man and woman, down to the poorest and most insignificant, was equally the object of God's love, and everyone counts, because God counts them,[1] then this, in political guise, led us to democracy and the involvement of the ordinary citizens in the framing of their laws. Writer John Lucas made the point:

> 'A decision is democratically taken if the answer to the question "who takes it?" is "more or less everybody", in contrast to decisions taken only by those best qualified to take them, as in meritocracy, or those taken by only one man, as in autocracy or monarchy. Secondly, democracy describes how a decision is reached. A decision is taken democratically if it is reached by discussion, criticism, and compromise. Thirdly,

democracy describes the spirit in which a decision is made, being concerned with the interests of all, instead of only a faction or party.'[2]

Intrinsic to democracy, above all other forms of government, is the importance of each individual as created and loved by God. It permits the examining, correcting and rebuking process, which is necessary in man's fallen and corruptible state, by emphasising that powerful officers of government are accountable to ordinary people. The Bible talks much of accountability both to and by authority, and democracy is the only form of government which permits the continual checking of centralising power. Through the ballot box, the Christian has the power to influence power structures and governments towards justice, freedom, truth and compassion, since governments can only rule by the consent of the people as they, in turn, examine the issues and arrive at a consensus.

God has displayed the doctrine of 'common grace' through three main social institutions – the family, the Church and the State. In free nations they permit the expression of individual conscience, the encouragement of good and the restraining of evil, enabling civil structure and social order to operate. There is always room for improvement within democratic structures. Universal suffrage, for example, would be wholly consistent with the Christian view of the family unit, which currently makes no representation to the State. The provision of the vote from birth, which would be exercised by the parents during the voter's years of minority, would be a natural extension of the principle of equality and give the family its rightful electoral status. Democracy would thereby be improved, and a crucial unit of society would have the power to participate in determining its own development and future. This may be the means of halting the modern madness of social experimentation, which risks the destruction of the family and will ultimately cause great damage to society. The family was God's first and most important social institution, bringing up the young and teaching them to live with other members of their own family and then society.

The institution of the State was also part of God's pattern for social life:

> *'Everyone must submit himself to the governing authority ... The authorities that exist have been established by God ... He is God's servant to do you good ... an agent of wrath to bring punishment on the wrongdoer.'*
>
> *(Romans 13:1, 4)*

God's will is to be done on earth as it is in heaven, and good government is intrinsic to that end.

> *'Give justice to the weak and the fatherless; maintain the right of the afflicted and the destitute. Rescue the weak and the needy; deliver them from the hand of the wicked.'*
>
> *(Psalm 82:3–4)*

It is the duty of government to govern righteously, and mete out varying levels of punishment on those who transgress the law.

The institution of the Church should be the most effective means of restraining evil. In being salt and light, the Church exists to turn the world's values upside down and bring people to an understanding of their creator, and eventually to an acknowledgement of the rule of God in their lives. The Reformed Church has been the instigator of enormous political reforms, as well as being responsible for producing some of the most influential scientists and philosophers over the last three centuries. History proves that the growth of liberty and the general progress of society have been intimately linked with the development of Judaism and Christianity. Such progress is inseparable from the

Judeo-Christian concept of God and its recognition that there is an eternal and objective moral law, rooted in God and reflecting His goodness. The gods of this world are concerned with the worship of power and the pursuit of pleasure and success; they encourage the fusion and concentration of temporal and spiritual power in the hands of the executive ruler. But biblical Christianity emphasises the superiority of God's Law over all kings, princes and authorities, and insists that the possession of power and responsibility at any level is a sacred trust, which should not be abused out of pride, vanity or personal gain. Its pivotal role in the struggles against torture, slavery, tyranny and inhumanity has often been obscured by both the slow pace of reform and by the human failings of Christian statesmen, theologians and denominations. Indeed, Christians have added to the sum of human cruelty whenever they have fallen prey to the temptation to use the power of the State to coerce the consciences of individuals. Instead, we should imitate the example of Jesus and the early Church by loving our enemies and combating error and heresy with the spiritual weapons of prayer, argument and evangelism.

## The democratic deficit

The principles of democracy are completely undermined by a European oligarchy where the supreme powers of state and government are in the hands of a small body of individuals – the Commissioners. This executive body of the Union meets in secret and initiates legislative proposals, some of which are put to the Council of Ministers. They are neither democratically elected nor under the direct control of elected politicians. They make decisions by majority vote, and are not accountable to any other body. The Council of Ministers is the law-making body and also meets in secret, again taking decisions by majority vote. The former vice-president of the European Parliament, Sir Fred Catherwood, observes:

> 'No-one outside knows how the arguments went, or even what arguments there were. There is no record of who voted for what, and the press have to be satisfied with unattributed and often conflicting official reports. If and when the legislation works its way back to national parliaments, it is presented to members who know very little about it, by a government minister who has already negotiated with fourteen other ministers a deal which he cannot alter. Such a process is not democracy. Democracy needs an open, on-the-record public debate – open to the press, and open to informed political comment. Then citizens can respond and tell their elected representatives what they think.'

His observations are wholly consistent with the proposition of oligarchical rule. Giles Chichester MEP has also attacked the absence of democracy. He said:

> 'The most fundamental contradiction lies in calling the Parliament a democratic body when its members are elected in so many different ways and represent such a hugely divergent number of electors. It is beyond me how anyone can describe a process, which gives disproportionate power to minority parties, encourages proliferation of parties, requires deal-making in private without reference to the electorate and abandons the constituency principle, as more democratic than our present system in the UK. There is far more transparency in our system where coalitions are formed before an election and expressed in a manifesto.'[3]

The European government machine is nothing to do with democracy and justice, and everything to do with power.

Since 1991, when Sir Fred made that observation, the *Maastricht Treaty* has actually extended the powers of the Council of Ministers. This in turn means that policy decisions which affect the United Kingdom are being taken by individuals who are not responsible to Britain or its electorate. For the 375 million citizens of the EU, all the decisions are taken by just 50 people: 15 heads of state and government, 15 ministers in Councils of Ministers, and 20 European Commissioners. None of these 50 has been elected by the people to carry out *European* government functions, and they are accountable to no-one for those functions. Many of the faces would be completely unknown to the people of Europe, and a more alarming fact is that neither the democratically elected European Parliament nor the national parliaments can overturn the decisions of these 50 oligarchs; European laws are absolute. This is not a secret agenda, but an openly admitted policy. As Bill Newton Dunn MEP stated in 1990:

> 'There is no plot by the European Parliament to usurp powers from the House of Commons. The Commons has never had power over European laws. When ministers go to Brussels, they leave their democratic shackles behind them.'[4]

The most threatening and the most federal of all the European institutions is the European Court of Justice. This Court is the final arbiter on matters relating to European law and has the power to overrule national, sovereign laws where these conflict with European aims. Judges are appointed to interpret the meaning of law and justice, and to do this they ought to consist 'from persons whose independence is beyond doubt and who possess the qualifications necessary required for appointment to the highest office in their respective countries.' However, in practice, the judges are a mixture of former judges, law professors, lawyers in private practice and government legal advisors. Many would fail to meet the criteria required to sit within the English courts. The fact that they owe their positions to the European government renders an obligation to work towards an 'ever closer union'. Indeed, this was enshrined in the *Treaty of Rome*, which clearly states that the European Court must 'ensure that in the interpretation and application of this treaty, the law is observed.'[5] Thus, those who are meant to guard the limits of State power do not have such primacy, but pass unlimited power into the hands of the legislature, thereby creating an element of totalitarianism in the State. Judgements of the 15 judges of the Court of the European Communities in Luxembourg have been set above those of the once highest appellate court in the House of Lords. Their judgements, driven by the treaty preamble to press for 'ever closer union', are unappealable. In the words of Sir Patrick Neil QC, former Warden of All Souls College, Oxford, such a politically active supreme court is a 'tyranny'. Evidence given to the House of Lords Committee claimed the European Court of Justice pursued a political policy which was 'incompatible with the democracy claimed for the *Treaty on European Union*.'

A former member of the European Commission, Claude Cheysson, stated that the Europe of Maastricht 'could only have been created in the absence of democracy.' Another former Commissioner, Raymond Barre, stated: 'I never understood why public opinion about European ideas should be taken into account.' Thus the last word on all European legislation lies with the bloc vote of the unrepresentative Council of Ministers. The façade of democracy is the European Parliament, to which member states elect their representatives. It is not democracy which is failing the citizens of Europe, but the degenerate systems which claim this title. If Satan can masquerade as an angel of light and demons appear as ministers of righteousness (*2 Corinthians 11:14*), then it is not so far removed from the realms of possibility that a system of government which hides behind a cloak of democracy is, in reality, nothing of the sort. Of course, the way in which the people participate in government will differ from country to country, and will be determined by history and tradition, but there are many ground rules of democracy which are being swept aside by the oligarchs of Europe. By operating behind something called a parliament, the Council of Ministers and the Commissioners are able to maintain the deception that democracy is being served and is supreme. The reality is rather different.

Up until the *Single European Act* in 1986, this body was called an assembly; its functions were to talk and debate. It is now incorrectly termed a parliament, though none of its powers have been increased. It has no legislative or tax-raising authority – it merely has the power to debate and make suggestions. With the passing of the *Single European Act*, huge areas of Britain's national sovereignty were given away by the enlargement of Europe's 'qualified majority voting' system. The appalling thing is that most MPs did not even notice. The debate on the Act was scheduled to begin on a Thursday – an unpopular time for most MPs, who normally journey back to their constituencies on a Friday. It continued through the night and over the weekend, until it was concluded. During these few nights, Britain transferred more of its sovereignty to the European Commission than it had all through the 1970s, and this under the leadership of one of Europe's fiercest critics, Margaret Thatcher. For a prime minister who was always thought to be in control, and who always seemed to know what was going on, the paradox must now be clear and painful. Even while she observed: 'The whole axis is France and Germany, and what they say the others agree with,'[6] she ardently pursued her monetarist policies and free market philosophy, believing the Act to be wholly consistent with and necessary for the fulfilment of her vision. In so doing, of course, she compromised Britain's sovereignty even further and was, in the words of one of her back-benchers, 'definitely conned'.[7]

A number of concerned MEPs wrote a booklet entitled *The Position of the European Parliament on Maastricht*. It listed no less than 22 'major shortcomings' of the new treaty.[8] Within its 68 pages, it refers to the undemocratic nature of the European Commission and the 'democratic deficit' of EC structures. However, national parliaments viewed the ratification of this treaty with considerable urgency and gave it top priority. Ironically, Sir Fred Catherwood urges Christians to look to the European Union as 'the way to a greater democracy', but completely ignores his own perceptions expressed in *Pro-Europe?*, as well as the expressed concerns of the democratically elected European Parliament, that the EU is anything but democratic. If Sir Fred's proposal is for the democratic United Kingdom to be subsumed by the undemocratic and federal European Union in the hope that the latter will evolve more democratic structures, then he is utterly misguided. He stated in 1991:

'Two Inter-Governmental Conferences are due to recommend the strengthening of the Community, first to make the present European monetary system an economic and monetary union, and second to strengthen the political institutions of the Community to make it more accountable and, we hope, a great deal more democratic.'

Note the order of these priorities: monetary union precedes greater democracy; the power of the exchequer has a higher priority than the voice of the people. Significantly, these hopes were voiced during the run-up to Maastricht, a treaty which certainly made huge progress on the issue of monetary union but did nothing to serve democracy. The observations of the former European Commissioner, Claude Cheysson, were correct. It is intolerable that people with legitimate and urgent complaints cannot look to those they elect for help and redress. Until the European Parliament becomes the legislature for the people of Europe, there is little hope of the people initiating any changes in law or putting right anything they believe has gone wrong. The case is overwhelming.

Democracy demands that sovereignty should rest in the hands of the people and be exercised by their representatives, to whom the administration (i.e. the European Commission) should be responsible. It is a fragile system of government, and can only work if people share enough in common to feel part of one community, so that minorities can accept majority decisions and live with the consequences. If, on the other hand, political differences are intensified by differences of language, nationality and culture, then minorities will regard majority rule as oppressive and are likely to rebel against it – and in so doing threaten civil peace. Although the architects of a federal Europe may believe EU member countries to be democracies sharing the heritage of Christendom, they ignore the many differences which would work against the formation of a multi-national state. There is a plethora of different languages, cultures and political traditions, and four of the countries concerned (Belgium, Greece, Italy and Germany) have only been unified nation states since the last century. Unlike Britain, most of them have known defeat and occupation in the recent past, and only Holland and Britain have enjoyed three centuries of peaceful, democratic parliamentary government under a constitutional monarchy. While no-one wishes to doubt the good faith or commitment to democracy of the present supporters of the EU, history proves that, human nature being what it is, the creation of a new and enlarged layer of government across national boundaries will increase the opportunities and temptations to abuse power. Even if the tyrannical tendencies of a future European government were no greater than those of a national one, the loss of freedom would be so widespread and serious that democracy would collapse. For a continent which has experienced civil wars, revolutions, communism, fascism, and is troubled by current Balkan tensions, this is not a remote prospect but a concerning reality.

## An 'ever closer union' – by stealth

It needs to be observed that since 1975, 'ever closer union' with our European neighbours has progressed with neither the consent of the British people nor a consensus as expressed through a referendum. The British people were previously consulted on the *economic* issue of trade, and membership of the European Economic Community (EEC). At the outset of campaigning, the nation was 2:1 against the proposal, but money for the pro-European campaign poured in – some £1.5 million – which dwarfed the meagre £133,000 managed by the anti-Europe campaign, spearheaded by politicians such as Enoch Powell and Tony Benn. So slick was the pro-Europe campaign that the nation was converted 2:1 in favour of the plan. Sir Teddy Taylor MP observed: 'The people were misled, conned and cheated.'[9] Meetings between Prime Minister Heath and President Pompidou of France had already put the issue of monetary union on the table – a fact which was never mentioned either to Parliament or to the nation. Enoch Powell spoke out vehemently, saying:

> 'I did not become a member of our sovereign Parliament to see that sovereignty abated or transferred.'[10]

From the other side of the House, Tony Benn defended the people's democracy, calling for them to be able to 'exercise the same basic right of self-determination.'[11]

While the White Paper on our EEC membership talked of a family of nations which would pool some of their sovereignty where necessary, and never against the will of any nation, the reality of the *Treaty of Rome* and the *Treaty of Maastricht* proved very different. 'Pooling' sovereignty actually dissolves it, since Britain can always be outvoted and overruled. However democratic the European Parliament may become, the reality is that British MEPs will always be a minority, and thus the right of self-government has been removed by the new European federal government. Even if Britain were to elect only Conservative MEPs, a Conservative government in the UK would still be subject to a European socialist government. This is the nature of the 'ever closer union' needed to lead to a superstate with one Government, one Parliament, and one overriding Court of Justice. As with most of the previous attempts to unify this continent, all these bodies would be tied to the Socialist-Catholic ethos of the majority of European nations. The former Labour Party cabinet minister Baroness Shirley Williams confirmed this observation during the run-up to the 1975 Referendum on Britain's continuing EEC membership. She said:

> 'We will be joined to a Europe in which the Catholic religion will be the dominant faith, and in which the application of the Catholic Social Doctrine will be a major factor in everyday political and economic life.' [12]

No matter what the Conservative Party may be telling Parliament and the electorate back home, in Brussels Conservative MEPs have a curious alliance with the openly federalist European People's Party (EPP), the federation of Christian Democrat Parties of the European Union. Since its foundation, the EPP has been strongly committed to the creation of a United States of Europe and has even gone so far as to draft a model constitution, to which the European Conservative group has become allied. As the *Financial Times* observed:

> 'Most Christian Democrats are keen Euro-federalists. Among such people, Mrs Thatcher is hardly the most popular European politician. The Tory MEPs had little chance of being admitted to the EPP group so long as she was leader.' [13]

For the European vision to proceed, she had to go. Since that time, Tory MEPs have set themselves an impossible balancing act. As one of their number, Lord Bethell, observed:

> 'We are expected to be Dr Jekylls, upholders of British interests who would go down with the ship rather than compromise, and Mr Hydes, ready to do deals with foreigners ... I heard Mr Major ... accusing Liberals and Labour of federalism, which was a "threat to our constitution". Then I heard him say on the eve of the actual day I joined the EPP, "I could never accept a federal Europe." I worked for his victory ... yet here I am, Mr Hyde again, the self-confessed federalist – a federast.' [14]

And Lord Tebbit commented:

> 'The EPP is a federalist party; it believes in a central European State in which Great Britain and the various other parts of the Community would be provinces. There would probably be a couple of English provinces and a Scottish and a Welsh province. Now that is totally and completely unacceptable, and yet our European Members of Parliament are allied to the EPP.'

Some Tory MEPs dismiss the contradiction. Sir Christopher Prout explained:

> 'Where there seems to be a division, it is often a question of vocabulary rather than substance.'[15]

However, *'the ear trieth words, as the mouth tasteth meat'* (*Job 34:3*), and such a point raises a very interesting issue. With the EPP committed to a federal Europe,[16] the establishing of a single currency with a single system of taxation, support for the Social Chapter in every country of the EU, support for a common defence with a European army, European control of Britain's nuclear weapons, and a European television broadcasting system, it is difficult to see how these are merely 'a question of vocabulary'. The very real 'substance' here is obvious and of profound significance, and many such policy commitments of the EPP are directly at odds with the stated aims of the Conservative Party.

The enthusiastic faces of federalism of the Labour and Liberal Democrat Parties, along with many Tories' concealed federalism, make it difficult to see how the British people can ever cast a vote opposing the formation of a federal state of Europe. Such a crucial absence of democracy has not been confined to Britain. In order to ratify the *Maastricht Treaty*, Belgium actually suspended her parliament's democratic process, thus avoiding debate, scrutiny and consultation. But Raymond Barre has confirmed that such a consultation process was never part of the plan; the Economic Community has had a momentum all of its own, changing and adapting like a chameleon to suit its ends, conveniently dropping the word 'Economic' when it wished to (creating overnight a new European Community), and evolving still further into the present European Union, which is more about political union than mere issues of trade. The European Court of Justice is a political court devoted, in its own words, to 'overcoming the resistance of national governments to European integration.' The British people have had no choice on this. Those who were elected to represent us are charged with the authority to legislate on our behalf on any matter but the power by which they legislate. As Lord Justice Megarry declared:

'As a matter of law, the Courts of England recognise Parliament as being omnipotent in all save the power to destroy its omnipotence.' [17]

Members of Parliament have given away to Brussels what was never theirs to part with. The sovereignty of Parliament is a cornerstone of Britain's unwritten constitution and is the essence of democratic tradition. Historically, it has been able to override previous legislation and pass new legislation at will – it could do anything except bind succeeding Parliaments. But the *Treaty of Maastricht*, as an irreversible and internationally enforceable treaty, has put an end to the sovereign prerogative of Parliament, and has placed democracy, civil liberty and national assets in the hands of the European Court of Justice.

In an EU official document on Maastricht, the following recommendation is made:

'The European Parliament should call for the application in full of the treaty and its provisions, but above all, seriously boost its efforts to introduce into the Union system a real federal-type constitution.' [18]

Bill Cash MP makes the further observation that the Commission has the exclusive right to initiate all legislation,[19] and that Maastricht extends the unaccountability of the EC decision-making process, removing power from the ordinary peoples throughout Europe, and shifting it to the remote Brussels bureaucracy. Bureaucrats are nothing like officials or civil servants. In theory, the latter have the function and duty of serving the public – they know what they have to do and are responsible to the community. They are not, therefore, anonymous cogs in a machine, but are supposed to be helpers and servers of their fellow citizens. Power for them is not an end in itself, but a means of fulfilling their social purpose. Bureaucrats, however, wield power for its own sake. The ideal of service vanishes in the face of the ability to order people about: the citizen is not a subject, but an object. Bureaucrats tend to regard themselves as masters rather than servants, and the anonymity of their functioning tends to keep power centralised in the department they represent. Controls over such administrations are necessary simply because it is difficult to appeal against their decisions: the increasing domination of the state permits them to create official positions for their followers, with salaries paid out of public funds, and dissenting voices are rapidly dispensed with.

The *Maastricht Treaty* confirms European bureaucratic supremacy over more than 70 policy areas, including taxation, monetary policy, education, immigration, judicial policy, health and safety, industrial policy, competition, regional policies, overseas aid, energy, and consumer affairs. It further commits the UK to the first two stages of monetary union. It does not take much to see that there is little else left for the British Parliament to legislate on. Since the right to veto legislation in any of these vital areas of national interest has been surrendered, the UK is moving inexorably towards nothing more than a façade of democracy. Tony Benn MP made a very salient point during the paving debate on the *Maastricht Bill*:

'One reason that we do not have many riots in Britain is that people can have a say. Over many years I have said, "Do not riot; vote. You can defeat the government in that way and you will achieve what you want

by peaceful means." People do not realise that democracy hangs on a very slender, delicate thread. If the
line is broken and people realise that no matter for
whom they vote in an election, decisions will be taken
by the European Union, I do not say they will riot, but
we could not argue against action taken directly by
them because there was no democratic route for the
solution to their problem.' [20]

Despite all the assurances being given by MPs, the
European Commission and Parliament are transforming
the Union into a federal constitution, which will make the
European oligarchy sovereign over every aspect of British
democracy. British politicians will soon no longer be the
representatives of the British people, but mere delegates of
Brussels.

## The bland leading the bland

One of the most curious features of the European Union is
the way in which it seems to mesmerise politicians to the
point of blindness. Trying to make coherent sense out of an
institution which operates through distorting mirrors is a
time-consuming and demanding process. Nothing is ever
quite what it seems, and few politicians are willing to expose
these distortions. Any confrontations which are made are
well-orchestrated 'Britain gets tough with Europe' postures,
but each round fought is a round where Britain's defeat is
fore-ordained.

'It is a case of the bland leading the bland, old lies piled
upon old lies, and useful idiots leading the country to
its destruction, without in many cases realising the true
state of affairs. Indeed, one of the most dispiriting
aspects of this tragedy is the Faustian pact so many
politicians have made in closing their minds to the

truth and allowing them to be swamped with distortions.'[21]

One bold Foreign Office and Treasury Minister, David Heathcote-Amory MP, did dare to challenge the direction of Government policy. On resigning, he wrote to the Prime Minister:

'I am leaving because I can no longer support the Government's policy on European Union ... I have dealt with the European Union at first hand. I have supported a policy of attempting to reform it and building a relationship which protects British interests and prevents unwarranted interference in our affairs. This policy is not working. The drive to political union in Europe is relentless and has already gone beyond what most people regard as acceptable.'

He further stated that the Government's equivocation on a single currency was unacceptable, but the most important sentence, from a man of considerable experience and standing, was the undeniable fact that British policy is *not working*.

Recent rows in policy have included the song and dance over the maximum working week, when the European Court of Justice overruled Britain's supposed opt-out of the Social Chapter of the *Maastricht Treaty*; the synthetic row over mad cow disease and the ensuing 'beef war'; the indignation over 'quota-hopping' and the imposition of reduced fish-catches for Britain in her own waters; and the possibility of huge fines being imposed if Britain pursues an economic policy which renders her more competitive than the Continent. Each instance has provided abundant entertainment for the tabloid newspapers, but in each confrontation British ministers have consistently failed to win any concessions at all. An imminent challenge by the

EU to Britain's border controls is likely to be a further defeat for the British Government, on the grounds of the Maastricht requirements for the free movement of people and goods. As the *Sunday Telegraph* observed:

> 'What this is about is the extent to which Britain is being smuggled into economic and monetary union by the back door, and it is remarkable just how secretive the Euro-establishment has been.' [22]

Bland British leadership through the European halls of distorting mirrors is facilitating the relentless moves for European political union. It is no longer easy to discern the blind from the bland. Kenneth Clarke was a leading proponent of the *Maastricht Treaty* while boasting that he had never bothered reading it. Blind he may be, but his aspiration has been confessed:

> 'I look forward to the day when the Westminster Parliament is just a Council Chamber in Europe.' [23]

So on the one hand, he grandly asserts that British taxpayers would not become liable for a £1.2 trillion bill for European unfunded pension debt, while Jacques Delors asserts:

> 'All members of EMU would become liable for the debts of a single country.' [24]

Who is to be believed? The 'Father of Maastricht' or a mere British Chancellor? In the light of other recent disagreements and contradictions, there is an all-too-uncomfortable sense that the answer is foreknown. Being marched to the top of the hill only to be disappointingly marched down again has been a monotonous tactic of government. One day *The Independent* asserts:

'Ministers will block European 48 hour week'[25]

and a week later *The Sunday Times* reports:

> 'The Government is having to draw up plans to implement the European demand for a 48 hour limit on the working week after a warning that ministers could be personally liable if they refuse.'[26]

Everything seems to be upside-down or back-to-front. If this is not blindness, it is certainly political dyslexia.

## 'Let us make Europe in our image'

John Major spoke at the Annual General Convention of the Institute of Directors in April 1996, when he stated:

> 'We are staying in Europe, but what kind of Europe? We aim to build a Europe that is more in our image.'

He failed to explain precisely how this would be achieved, given the impediment that the other EU members would have to agree, either by majority or unanimity, with the British concept of European co-operation. If his 'image' is anything like that of John Redwood MP, the former contender for the leadership of the Conservative Party, then it will demand that the UK should

> 'grasp the agenda in Brussels and insist on a Europe of freer trade and more jobs, rather than the Europe of the ERM, over-regulation and the dole queue. We should argue for stronger links with the countries of Eastern Europe, for a free trade area of the North Atlantic, and for measures to remove the obstacles to more jobs in Europe.'

Redwood concludes:

> 'It is Britain's task to save Europe from herself.'

This aspiration reveals many of the misconceptions and much of the ignorance which is clouding political thought. The EU is a collective, and it is simply not possible to 'grasp the agenda' of a collective. The agenda of this particular collective is set by the Committees of Permanent Represent- atives serving the Council of Ministers, and the European Commission. The agenda cannot be 'grasped' by one member state, any more than one member state can 'insist' on something. A number of MPs have been calling for a renegotiation of the *Maastricht Treaty*, believing they can divert the European train from its single-direction rail track, but in a collective no member of it can re-orientate the direction in which it is travelling. A Europe of freer trade means a Europe without the Common Agricultural Policy, and Britain has been 'insisting' for decades that this mechanism needs reform, without success. In a collective, a member can argue, insist or demand until he is blue in the face, but if his arguments do not prevail, the only way forward is to either leave the collective, or meekly accept the decisions of the collective which are anathema to him. This has been Britain's recent experience on many issues: insist, argue, jump on high horse, fail to convince the collective, then accept the collective decisions, regardless of the adverse economic, social and political consequences. A civil servant, writing to the *European Journal* in April 1996, clearly understood this:

> 'It is time for plain speaking on Europe. The fact is that Britain, in spite of its opt-out on monetary union and in spite of its increasingly vocal Euro-sceptics, is today sleep-walking into a European superstate from which there will be no escape short of civil war, bloodier even

than the Yugoslav fracas. The train of events leading to this momentous result is already in motion. There is still just time for Britain to jump off, but it is virtually now or never.'[27]

The *Single European Act* of 1986 and the *Maastricht Treaty* have procured the collectivisation of 'national interests' (except, in theory, in respect of issues which can be defended by the use of the national veto). It is now for the collective 15, plus the Commission, to decide what the interests of the collective may be, and for the member countries to put up with the collective's decision.

## Rule Britannia? Europa waives the rules

It is the assertion of Euro-manipulators that the notion of Britain having an absolute and inviolable sovereignty could only be taken seriously by 'Little Englanders'. They are accused of hankering after past glories and still appearing to think they live in 1897, when the Empire and British military and economic strength really did rule the waves. Such patronising assertions only serve to deflect attention from the real issues, and obscure completely the clandestine procedures of European legislation. Rodney Atkinson, a pro-nation activist, has recently highlighted the means by which European treaties have dispensed with national laws:

'The European legislation of 1972, 1986 and 1993 – swept through the British Parliament on a tide of ignorance and intimidation of MPs – was based on two unprecedented constitutional procedures: firstly, the use of international treaties to negotiate the *internal* constitution of the United Kingdom; secondly, the general transfer by our Parliament of powers to the European Community which then legislates specifically within the United Kingdom by directive and regulation, *which the British Parliament is powerless to resist.* The transfer of general powers to the State to act without the sanction of Parliament is precisely how Adolf Hitler gained such absolute power through his emergency laws.'[28]

The EU's riding roughshod over national law has not been confined to Britain. In Denmark, the ratification of the *Maastricht Treaty* is being scrutinised by constitutional courts. After three referenda, there is much unease with the potential future impositions which the treaty permits. Following Belgium's suspension of democracy to impose the treaty by decree, their government has also recently amassed powers to determine economic policy by decree. As this makes clear, the forces driving the European collective simply amend rules to suit their purposes, and are quite prepared to act illegally if necessary.

## References

1. *The Christian in Politics*, Walter James, 1962, OUP.
2. *Democracy & Participation*, John R Lucas, 1975, Pelican.
3. *The House Magazine*, 22nd January 1997.
4. *The House Magazine*, 19th November 1990.
5. *Treaty of Rome*, Articles 164–188.
6. Fontainebleau Summit, 1984.
7. Sir Teddy Taylor on *The Poisoned Chalice*, BBC2, 23rd May 1996.
8. *Maastricht: A Christian Dilemma*, Graham Wood, Campaign for an Independent Britain, 1992.
9. Sir Teddy Taylor, *The Poisoned Chalice*, BBC2, 16th May 1996.
10. Conservative Party Conference, 13th October 1971.
11. Labour Party Conference, 2nd October 1972.
12. Catholic Guild meeting, London, 1973–75 EEC membership campaign.
13. *Financial Times*, 8th April 1992.
14. *The Confessions of a True Blue 'Federast'*, Lord Bethell (MEP 1979–1984), *Daily Telegraph*, 27th April 1992.
15. Sir Christopher Prout MEP (1979–94), *Conservative Newsline*, May 1992, Conservative Central Office.
16. *Manifesto for the European Elections 1989*, EPP.
17. Blackburn v Attorney General, 1983.

18. *The Position of the European Parliament*, 20th–21st January 1992.
19. *Europe – The Crunch*, Bill Cash MP, The European Foundation.
20. House of Commons Official Report, *European Communities Bill*, 2nd December 1992.
21. *International Currency Review*, Vol. 23, No. 4, Autumn 1996.
22. *Sunday Telegraph*, 10th November 1996.
23. *International Currency Review*, Vol. 23, No. 4, Autumn 1996.
24. Speech to the European Parliament, 24th February 1995.
25. *The Independent*, 2nd July 1996.
26. *The Sunday Times*, 7th July 1996.
27. William Kenway (pseudonym), *European Journal*, April 1996.
28. *International Currency Review*, Vol. 23, No. 4, Autumn 1996.

# Chapter 5

# Citizenship

*'And Paul said, "I was born a free citizen." '*

*(Acts 22:28)*

The Apostle Paul, born a Roman citizen, was able to invoke the inherent freedoms afforded by that privilege. Although citizenship may be bought, adopted or voluntarily relinquished, those who enjoy the privileges of being born a free citizen in a free nation are not usually going to readily surrender them. Citizenship is inextricably linked to the nation state. Those who have British citizenship are defined by belonging within the borders of the United Kingdom, possessing the Union Jack as a national symbol and 'God save the Queen' as a national anthem, enjoying the right to carry a British passport, and being subject to British laws as passed by Parliament and given Royal assent. The development of a new citizenship which has been imposed on British nationals has been effected through prerogative power with unknown, evolving consequences.

## Citizens of Europe

Since the *Maastricht Treaty* of 1992, a common European citizenship has been established. It includes a single European flag, Beethoven's 'Ode to Joy' as a national anthem, borders as defined by the union of nations, the requirement to carry a new European passport and laws which take precedence over British Acts of Parliament. It would be difficult to argue coherently against the federal implications of these symbols of statehood. In 1992, Enoch Powell stated:

'What the EEC is bent upon has nothing to do with free trade or free anything. It is a naked assertion of the will to power, the will to create a unified state to which, instead of our own national organs of representation and government, we are all to be subordinated.' [1]

If other European nations are 'foreign', then none has the right to impose its citizenship upon a citizen of the UK. It would be an illegal invasion of democratic rights and unconstitutional.

The whole notion of dual citizenship becomes muddied in the extreme when a national parliament denies democracy and self-determination to its people by permitting an *obligatory* citizenship to be imposed by a foreign state. In the EU document *A Citizen's Europe*, there is confirmation of the duality. It states:

'Now that the Community is turning into a Union, a third set of rights and duties is coming into being, creating a European citizenship separate and distinct from national citizenship; not taking its place but supplementing it.' [2]

Citizenship of a new supra-national state may be permissible, even desirable to some, until they scrutinise the finer details of the consequences of such citizenship. The 'rights and duties' of citizens are further mentioned in the *Maastricht Treaty*, which states that citizens of the Union are 'subject to the duties imposed thereby'.[3] As one booklet on the subject observes:

> 'What are these duties? A close scrutiny of the treaty, and indeed other EC documents on the subject, fails to define them in any way. It is incomprehensible that legal minds responsible for framing and negotiating the treaty should fail to clarify such an important point affecting the lives of some 375 million European Citizens.'[4]

But fail they did; or was it that they purposely omitted such a definition in order to proceed by stealth and to define the implications of citizenship in successive treaties?

As more of Parliament's sovereignty is transferred to Brussels, the concept of belonging to the British State is increasingly eroded. Economic and monetary policy have already gone, and foreign and defence policy are soon to disappear, followed by home rule and social policy. Successive treaties will clarify the 'duties' and obligations of each citizen. It is not unreasonable to assume that eventually the European Commission and Council of Ministers will legally be able to commit the Union to war and impose conscription on its citizens, despite any conflict with British Acts of Parliament. All this could be done without any degree of accountability to the people. This is not so far-fetched when one considers the fragility of some British laws, which would be overruled if ever they were laid before the European Court of Justice. The *Act of Settlement* of 1701, forbidding Roman Catholic accession to the throne, would be ruled as bigoted and sectarian; the inequality between the heterosexual and homosexual ages of consent would be ruled as discriminatory and an infringement of civil liberties; and the blasphemy laws could well be extended to cover all faiths, making it effectively illegal to proclaim the supremacy of Jesus over any other god.

## Consequences for Christians

There is a steady stream of human-rights cases being brought to the attention of the European Parliament, many of them involving persecuted Christians in Asia or the Middle East who have been arrested for meeting together, proselytisation or failing to register officially as a church. It sometimes takes only one semi-political statement by a church leader for the police to be sent in. Those who have prayed for decades for the persecuted believers of Eastern Europe will doubtless be rejoicing at the new liberties which many of those countries now enjoy, but Christians who believe that God entrusted his creation to men and women must also believe that each generation has the duty to hand it on to the next generation in better shape than they found it. Much of what passes for the embryonic European Constitution is wholly humanist in content, and asserts that in a multi-faith society, Christian beliefs cannot be the foundation of law or custom. The Evangelical Alliance notes that Evangelical Christians are perceived by the EU as a 'sect', and that any group which does not belong to the majority church (Roman Catholic) is viewed by many MEPs with suspicion. This classification is nothing new. The Early Church was branded an heretical sect, and this was the earliest basis of persecution (*Acts 24:5, 14, 28:22*), a fact which ought to alarm members of evangelical 'sects' throughout Europe. Of course, any impending persecution will not be on overtly religious grounds: an enlightened EU would consider that abhorrent. Persecution will be political, as it was with the Early Church, with accusations of 'disturbing the peace' or 'inciting sectarianism' (*Acts 16:20ff, 17:7*). This tactic has been frequently employed throughout history, and continues to be employed by some oppressive regimes today, notably Chinese communists. But it is also emerging on British shores. In 1994, two open-air preachers were arrested in Bournemouth and held for 48 hours in police custody. In 1995, an open-air preacher was attacked in Gloucester. Although the police knew the attackers, they made no arrest. A Christian newsletter reports of one Christian couple who were arrested after speaking of Christ to a member of a religious street procession who had approached them. And there have recently been reports that the police have asked a church in a predominantly Muslim area to remove a Gospel text from their noticeboard.

David Hallam MEP has confirmed that a European resolution on sects and cults permits the European police force (Europol) to carry out surveillance on such groups' activities. He adds:

'In Europe, this could include Christians.'[5]

Whereas most MEPs have said there is no threat to 'bona fide religions' (*institutionalised* churches), during the debate on this resolution, one speaker did lump Evangelicals in with Satanists – a fact which demonstrates that the ramifications of this resolution are serious. The European Evangelical Alliance stated in response:

'We would object if policemen turned up on Sunday mornings at our services to check on what we were doing, but that would be a possibility in some European countries. We would like British Christians to pray about this situation.'

For Britain, a nation which has been proud of its freedom of speech and which long ago banished religious persecution from its shores, there is a very real threat in a Socialist-Catholic Europe which undermines centuries of hard-won liberties and which may be sowing the seeds of future social discontent. The subtle erosion of citizenship and the diminution of the nation state itself may seem a relatively unimportant occurrence, especially when placed in the context of a world of starvation, war and untold suffering and persecution, but it is worth remembering that citizenship and nationalism have been at the root of the Bosnian conflict; these issues are central to Quebec's attempts at secession from the Canadian federation; they are the reasoning behind the pleas for Scottish devolution; and the nexus of civil wars within the former Soviet Union. The current world story is of nations trying to liberate themselves from artificially created nation states – history proves they simply do not work. When one examines the consequences of the terms of surrender imposed on Germany's Weimar Republic by the Allied nations following World War I, it is obvious that obligations imposed on patriotic citizens by foreigners, and the lessening of the standing of the nation state, can lead to all manner of extreme expressions of nationalism which eventually result in war against the perceived oppressor. Christian believers who wish to learn from recent history and counsel their leaders against such dangerous possibilities have an obligation to use their democratic votes wisely.

## Constitutional liberties

It seems curious that the entire European unification process is continuing in light of the fact that two world wars this century were fought to oppose the forces of a European hegemony and to defend independence, democracy and freedom. The European hegemony now so ardently being pursued by politicians is, in reality, no different from that which was pursued by Charlemagne, Napoleon or Hitler, though the centralising process this time is happening beneath the democratic mantle of treaties and negotiations, instead of by force of arms. As the world becomes smaller, more accessible and more interdependent, there are those who view Britain's membership of the EU as a necessity, if Britain is to maintain any degree of influence in global affairs. The magnitude of the trading bloc to which a nation belongs seems to be the sole determining factor in this reasoning, and the leverage the bloc can exert on other trading alliances through taxes, tariffs, embargoes or free trade is somehow proportional to its political influence in global affairs. Of course, economic matters in an inter-connected world demand a degree of pooled sovereignty, but such co-operation does not need to infringe a nation's right to be autonomous and act in its own self-interest. Citizens should be free to order their own affairs through the process of democracy and the sovereignty of Parliament, otherwise those citizens are no longer free. Enoch Powell observed in 1992:

> 'A nation is free externally in the sense that all laws, policies, and acts of government generally which affect its citizens are made by its own institutions. In a nation "free" in this sense, no laws will be made, or taxes imposed, or judgements judged by an external author-ity ... but the UK is not free, since its laws may now be defined, its taxes imposed, and its policies laid down by an external authority, namely the institutions of the EC (now the EU).'[6]

The lack of political accountability and democratic justi-fication for the EU's federal aspirations, and the transferring of powers away from national parliaments to a centralising core, is anti-freedom, undemocratic and unconstitutional. Since each successive treaty has been concerned with the amalgamation of power into a centralised, unaccountable body, Christians should be all the more wary. The clear teaching of Scripture is that man's heart is inherently sinful; his natural inclination is towards greed, lust and power. The more these appetites are fed, the more is desired, and this observation has been confirmed time and again as the EU has evolved. Each gain has led to further demands, each concession to further erosion of national sovereignty. Even where Britain has an opt-out clause, the Commission seeks to impose its policy by other means as, for example, was shown by the debate over Maastricht's Social Chapter – which is now being imposed under the compulsory Health and Safety directives. The Union is a creation of law, and is now an autonomous law-making body in its own right, with full and final authority over its citizens. British national law is now subordinate to European law, and a further aspect of Britain's written constitution has been dispensed with – the 1689 *Bill of Rights* which enshrines the principle that no other power but the Queen-in-Parliament can make or amend British laws.

## Treason at Maastricht

The Chairman of the Freedom Association, Norris McWhirter, wrote to the Speaker of the House of Commons, Betty Boothroyd MP, setting out the constitutional case for her intervention during Parliament's ratification of the *Maastricht Treaty* in 1992. His incisive reasoning was centred around six areas where this treaty conflicted with both the law of the Constitution and the law of Parliament, and is quoted in full in Appendix 1. The Speaker's response, via a member of her staff, constituted nothing more than a courtesy letter, thanking him for his 'interesting observations'. McWhirter was dismayed that even the Speaker – whose duty is to uphold democracy – would not act. One of the most significant treasonable aspects of the treaties of Rome and of Maastricht concerns the constitutional position of the Monarch. During her reign, Queen Elizabeth I stated:

> 'To no power whatsoever is my crown subject save to that of Christ the King of Kings.'

Section Three of the *Treason Felony Act* of 1848 asserts that condemnation is incurred

> 'If any person whatsoever shall, within the United Kingdom or without, compass, imagine, invent, devise or intend to deprive or depose our most gracious Lady the Queen ... from the style, honour, or royal name of the imperial crown of the United Kingdom.'

The punishment for convicted offenders is life imprisonment, yet not a finger has been lifted against the Privy Counsellors, Douglas Hurd and Francis Maude. These two signed the *Maastricht Treaty* which, at a stroke, brought the Queen under the suzerainty of the European Union and thereby made her a citizen of that Union. Now that she is a citizen of a different political entity and is subject to past and future judgements of the Court of the European Communities in Luxembourg, from which there is no appeal, her role as a constitutional monarch has been put into doubt. By the treaty, this Court has been confirmed in authority over her courts, in which she was not previously arraignable.[7] Her new status as a citizen of the EU has rendered her, like the rest of the British people, 'subject to the duties imposed thereby'. The Privy Counsellor's Oath, which Hurd and Maude had sworn, is a promise 'To bear faith and allegiance to the Crown and to defend its jurisdiction and powers against all foreign ... persons ... or states.' There can be no doubt that both Hurd and Maude have breached this oath. The seven charges of treason which have been levelled against the co-signatories of the treaty were deemed by the Director of Public Prosecutions, Dame Barbara Mills, to be sound in law. They were submitted to the Attorney General, under whose superintendence she works. But as a judge in his own cause, he obviously ruled that there should be no further action.

The whole case has thus been sat upon and silenced, and no publicity was given to it at the time.

The four great constitutional statutes for British citizens – the *Magna Carta* of Edward I (1215), the *Petition of Right* (1627), the *Bill of Rights* (1689) and the *Act of Settlement* (1701) – have never been expressly repealed, though successive European treaties imply that they have been repealed. There is a profound dilemma here for the Christian, since it is not possible to serve two masters. Either he submits to British law and protests that obedience to it must imply a breaking of European law, or he decides to treat European law as supreme on all matters and ignores British law, which is, by treaty implication, redundant. It is a very ominous dilemma, for the implications of the constitutional change have not yet become a subject of wide debate and there is a high level of ignorance, if not apathy, towards the whole subject. Christians in pursuit of unity, peace and compromise would rather bury their heads in the sand and propose obedience to the authorities than address such an unprecedented loss of freedom and disregard for the nation's Christian heritage, if only because the issue is seen as too remote and is a problem which belongs to tomorrow in any case. The seeds of deep resentment and civil disorder are much easier to eliminate at this stage than they will be when grown to maturity, but they are far harder to identify. The dilemma for British citizens has been incisively encapsulated by Enoch Powell:

'New authorities have been called into existence to supersede the Parliament of this Kingdom and to define and enforce new rights and liberties. What remains to be seen is whether "the people of this Kingdom" accept those authorities. If they do, they have lost their "true ancient and indubitable rights and liberties" and acquired none in exchange. Not even the French in 1789 did that.'[8]

It is time that Britain woke up to the fact that, like thieves in the night, the Eurocrats and their collaborators have stolen British sovereignty and liberty, and have given nothing in exchange.

## *References*

1. *Enoch Powell on 1992*, edited by Richard Ritchie, Anaya Publishers Ltd.
2. *A Citizen's Europe*, Pascal Fontaine, EC Publications Unit.
3. *Maastricht Treaty*, Article 8:2.
4. *Maastricht: A Christian Dilemma*, Graham Wood, CIB, 1992.
5. *IDEA magazine*, The Evangelical Alliance, June–August 1996.
6. *Enoch Powell on 1992*, edited by Richard Ritchie, Anaya Publishers Ltd.
7. *Freedom Today*, Norris McWhirter, June 1996.
8. *Enoch Powell on 1992*, edited by Richard Ritchie, Anaya Publishers Ltd.

# Chapter 6

# Monetary Union

*'For the love of money is the root of all evil.'*

(*1 Timothy 6:10*)

Money is supposed to make the world go round. Certainly those who control the world's money supplies are at the helm of global destiny; determining who owes what to whom, which nations prosper, which nations endure crippling interest rates, which nations are bribable, which continents can be controlled by monetary intervention and which regimes will fall because of economic hardships. Money influences every aspect of life through government or independent banking policy – money and power are bedfellows in all walks of life. Those who have plenty find it easy to lord it over those who have little, and those who have little or none are beholden to those who become their creditors. It is the same principle, from individual trans-actions to global power-play – he who holds the purse strings has the ultimate authority.

The debate over the independence of the Bank of England is essentially a debate about the control of infla-tion, and has convincing arguments on both sides. Inflation is certainly a moral issue because it is, in reality, a fraud policy implemented by a government which hits the poorer members of society disproportionately. Since the Queen's head first appeared on British coins and notes in 1952, their value has decreased by over 90 per cent – the fastest and most persistent rate of inflation Britain has ever had. This devaluation has not occurred during years of war or economic hardship, but during great prosperity when, it is said, Britain has 'never had it so good'. At least some of this may be attributed to the fact that British political parties are free to give themselves a better chance of re-election by engineering a pre-election boom, which the short-sighted electorate eventually has to pay for in recession, inflation and high interest rates. The attractions of an independent Bank of England seem, therefore, to be self-evident, but it does not necessarily follow that joining a Europe-wide monetary system is in Britain's best interests.

## 'Thou art Euro, and on this Euro I will build Europe'

On 15th December 1995, the EU's leaders agreed that the intended single currency would be called the 'Euro'. The Spanish finance minister of the day, Pedro Solbes, made a play on Jesus' words to the Apostle Peter about building the Church by affirming that the Euro would be the very foundation of a united Europe.[1] This remark needs to be evaluated in the context of the EU's past use of a poster of the Tower of Babel, over which the EU flag's circle of stars are displayed in the inverted form of a pentagram. It was used by the Council of Europe to promote 'European construction'. These biblical images and allusions are becoming more commonplace, though the symbolism and significance are often perverted.

Within the context of the EU, the inexorable drive towards monetary union and the formation of a single currency has become the embodiment of the European superstate ideal and the culmination of the process to unify the European market. As Belgian Prime Minister Jean-Luc

Dehaene put it: 'Monetary union is the motor of European integration.' The implications are immense, for a single currency would require a single monetary policy, and the oversight and implementation of such a policy would be vested in one single decision-making body. This implies the evolution in one form or another of a European government, and demands a European Central Bank. A possible 80 per cent of Britain's reserves – some £22 billion – would be permanently handed over to such a bank, and the transfer would be irrevocable.

Many cheers of victory were heard in the Commons in 1992, when John Major negotiated the British opt-out to the latter stages of monetary union, but Bill Cash MP rightly believes that because of the sheer momentum of events, it is unlikely that the opt-out could be exercised. He said:

> 'The *Maastricht Treaty* commits us to the practical implications of having the whole Treasury, the Bank of England and the Civil Service machinery setting up the European Monetary Institute. It is incredible that the gravitational pull of this would allow us to stand aside at the last minute.'[2]

Articles in the treaty require all members of the EU collective to co-operate on an open-ended basis and not to take any steps which might impede the objectives of the collective. Britain is therefore treaty-bound, as all the other EU member states, to co-operate enthusiastically in preparing for the abolition of the national currency as a prelude to the abolition of the nation itself.[3] If the possibility that Britain may opt out of EMU participation had any meaning at all, it would be sensible for the Bank of England and the Treasury to have established a parallel working party to design the precise technical monetary arrangements which would emerge in London after Britain had said 'No'. The absence of such a working party is further proof that the designers of the EMU arrangements have assumed that no European country will be able or permitted (due to its treaty obligations) to resist ultimate incorporation within EMU, and thus the final loss of its sovereignty. Timings of entry may differ, but even those nations which remain temporarily outside EMU will not be able to go it alone. According to the Bundesbank:

> 'The European System of Central Banks, consisting of the ECB and the "national central banks" of the participating countries, will conduct its monetary policy operations in Euro right from the start of Stage Three ... at the *irrevocably fixed* conversion rates.'[4]

There is no mention of those non-participating nations whose rates of exchange may be driven by market factors and may consequently have a competitive advantage. The Bundesbank will not consider the possibility of any EU country remaining permanently outside EMU, since to do so is precluded by the obligations imposed by the *Maastricht Treaty*. The 'opt-out', about which the Prime Minister John Major has boasted for years, is to a large extent a misleading ruse for public consumption, since once the Euro is created, sterling's exchange rate with the Euro will be tied irrevocably. This is the precise reason that he has been going to extraordinary lengths to emphasise the 'necessity' for Britain to 'remain involved' in the EMU negotiations 'right up to the last moment'. This necessity arises from the text of the *Maastricht Treaty*, not from the Prime Minister's sense of public duty. Looking forward to 2003, Jacques Santer has said: 'There will be monetary union and Britain will be a member'[5] – no mention of an opt-out there.

According to the treaty, the European Central Bank would be independent of EU institutions and the governments of member states. This would, in turn, mean that the entire economic and fiscal policy of the United Kingdom would be put into the hands of a group of unelected and unaccountable European bankers. This concentration of power in an anonymous élite, which would meet and work behind closed doors, presents a host of potential dangers. Such a body would be a formidable power base, and able to influence political events to suit its own agenda: absolute power still corrupts absolutely. A Labour MP, Llew Smith, observes:

> 'A single currency will oblige Britain to become a member of the European Central Bank, the executive of which will be appointed for eight years. No matter what damage they inflict on us, no-one will be able to remove them ... People will still have the right to vote, but that vote will be a gesture – a charade – because the parties and governments for whom they vote will no longer have the powers to rectify the wrongs inflicted on them.'[6]

In the House of Commons on 25th November 1996, Kenneth Clarke sought to defuse the situation. He said:

> 'Unless we join Stage Three of economic and monetary union, we shall retain, as now, control of domestic economic policy.'

But only one interpretation can be placed upon that: that if we did join, we would no longer have control of our domestic policy.

This inordinate shift of power runs contrary to every democratic instinct and principle of liberty, and it elevates the power of central bankers above that of the elected legislature. The control of money is at the core of politics, self-government and sovereignty itself. The monarch's head upon a nation's currency is a symbol of that sovereignty: if a denarius (a Roman coin) bears the head of Caesar, then it belongs to Caesar; if sterling bears the head of the Queen, then her authority in Parliament is absolute; if the Euro bears the insignia of the European Union, then it should be rendered unto the European government because it will belong to the European government. Gladstone, writing in 1891, saw that money and power are inseparable bedfellows. He said:

> 'The finance of the country is ultimately associated with the liberties of the country. It is a powerful leverage by which the English liberty has been gradually acquired. If the House of Commons by any possibility loses the power of the control of the grants of public money, depend upon it, your very liberty will be worth very little in comparison. That powerful leverage has been what is commonly known as the power of the purse – the control of the House of Commons over public expenditure.'[7]

A European Central Bank with one economic policy and one interest rate would inevitably lead to federal taxation. As John Redwood MP observes, the European reasoning would be that

> 'to make it work we must impose higher taxes on the successful parts to send money to the poorer parts; to have a fair single market, now we have a fair single currency, we must have common taxation so one part cannot undercut another.'[8]

No-one is saying that Britain should be selfish with its wealth – it is incumbent upon all the wealthier nations of Europe to provide aid to the poorer members, as they are already doing. However, compulsory taxation at a European level is not the way forward. It is leaning towards

Communism. Christianity talks of freely giving with a cheerful heart – 'what's mine is yours'. Communism, on the other hand, asserts common ownership – 'what's yours is mine' – and has nothing to do with loving your neighbour or caring for the poor. Indeed, the Bible asserts that giving should not be under compulsion (*2 Corinthians 9:7*). The 'ever closer union', however, has profoundly concerning designs for massive taxation without representation, all in the name of 'fairness'.

## The silenced protests

There are many prominent business leaders who have openly voiced their opposition to EMU, though the media has rarely reported them. Sir Alick Rankin CBE warned:

> 'To join EMU – and abandon forever our sterling heritage – we must meet tough convergence criteria, pay up a huge "entrance fee" and put on a monetary corset. The ERM is a painful and recent memory – have we forgotten everything and learned nothing?'[9]

Timothy Melville-Ross, the Director General of the Institute of Directors, affirms:

> 'The retention of a domestic monetary policy is the only chance business has to enjoy low inflation and low interest rates.'[10]

A winner of the Queen's Award for Export Achievement, Sir Emanuel Kaye CBE, observes:

> 'A glance at Britain's trade figures should be enough to warn us of the dangers of favouring economic integration with Europe over our world-wide links. 56 per cent of our exports go outside the EU. Last year, Britain's

trade surplus of £15.74 billion with the rest of the world was wiped out by a £16.45 billion deficit with Europe.'[11]

And contradicting those who assert that foreign investors in Britain are encouraging our path to monetary union, the Japanese deputy chairman of Nikko Securities says:

'Japanese investors would actually prefer Britain to stay outside the single currency, so that their production bases here continue to enjoy the benefits of a competitive exchange rate. In fact, the interests of Japanese investors are identical to those of British exporters.'[12]

The predictions that inward investment would dry up if Britain remained outside EMU are clearly erroneous. Even with the British EMU opt-out position, and the Europe issue causing major divisions in British politics, Britain remains a favourite for massive inward investment. This was demonstrated on 11th July 1996, when a South Korean electronics company invested £1.7 billion in a new manufacturing plant, the largest ever single investment into Europe. There are also many small businesses who believe their success has been achieved *in spite* of EU membership, not because of it. In the words of the chairman of the Dixons Group plc, Sir Stanley Kalms:

'Business must now gird its loins and fight with every weapon. We must defend ourselves – up to the figurative barricades if necessary – against those who seek to sell out the UK to a federal Europe.'[13]

Even the Governor of the Bank of England, Eddie George, has gone public in his views. *The Times* of 15th May 1996 cited his rejection of the argument that Britain would suffer damage by remaining outside a single European currency.

## ERM powerplay

In December 1995, Professor Walter Eltis brought to the attention of the media what is blindingly obvious to many. He said:

> 'There are those who naively suppose that exchange-rate stability with the leading European currencies would remove all exchange-rate uncertainty, with consequent benefits to British business. The elimination of exchange-rate movements between sterling and the DM and the French franc would accentuate the degree of fluctuation between sterling and the dollar and the yen. To much of British industry, including some of Britain's most successful sectors, the sterling–dollar rate is what matters most.'

Yet the fixation with the Exchange Rate Mechanism, and the 'son' of ERM, continues to preoccupy the Treasury. During Britain's dabbling with the ERM in 1992, many distinguished economists who were opposed to the formation of a single currency made their views known. Professor Sir Alan Walters, personal economic adviser to Margaret Thatcher, was derided by the press for contradicting Nigel Lawson on the issue of shadowing the deutschmark. He foresaw the loss of financial control; that Britain would be bound by German domestic policy, and he rightly observed the relief of being able to leave the ERM, saying:

> 'If there had been one currency in operation there would have been no respite from the dominant German monetary squeeze ... The idea that a complete economic union necessarily requires a monetary

union has been widely accepted, however, by Euro-enthusiasts. This is an astonishing feat of public relations and press management by Brussels and its allies.' [14]

John Major also had a fixation with the ERM, and seemed prepared to inflict all manner of privation on the British people to cling to the policy. If it had not been possible to leave the torture, the ERM would have condemned more firms to closure, more workers to unemployment and more families to homelessness through unprecedented levels of repossession. How can the abdication to foreign control of the responsibility for these fundamental human needs ever be justified from a Christian perspective? God cares for the poor, the oppressed, and the underdogs in society. He pours His wrath over those who corrupt justice or create economic machines designed to provide more wealth for the wealthy and deprive the poor. The story of Naboth's vineyard in *1 Kings 21* establishes that authorities are not free to pursue any policy they please or to ride roughshod over the rights of the poor. These same concerns are vehemently expressed by the prophets Amos, Hosea, Isaiah and Micah, writing in the 8th century BC. God demands conscience above political conviction, and a superstate which places economic considerations above liberty and justice is guilty of worshipping Mammon above the Lord.

Through all the turmoil which led to Britain's withdrawal from the ERM, every interest rate increase was presented as a 'caring' gesture by John Major to his European 'partners' to maintain exchange rate parity and conform to the ERM rules. The total number of suicides, heart attacks, divorces and mental breakdowns which the policy directly or indirectly produced is unknown. Since 'Black Wednesday' (or should it be more appropriately known as 'White Wednesday'?), Britain has been free to pursue a monetary policy with British economic interests in mind. For all its continuing faults, at least it is a British system, and the British people can exercise their democratic rights and change it if they wish. Such pursuit of a domestically orientated policy is branded 'anti-European' by Britain's 'partners'. It is bad enough, according to Jacques Delors, that Britain's opt-out of the Social Chapter makes the country 'a paradise for foreign investment' [15] – an accurate enough observation. If Britain were 'left out' of monetary union, direct foreign investment would continue to flow in because of its market-friendly, outward-looking, non-protectionist, politically stable environment. Yet there is something about this which Chancellor Kohl will not tolerate. He ominously, almost arrogantly, warns:

> 'No-one in Europe – and I repeat, no-one – should labour under the illusion that he is in a position to go it alone.' [16]

Although the current British Chancellor, Kenneth Clarke, maintains favour for a single currency, one of his 'wise men', Professor Patrick Minford, argues:

> 'A stagnant, protected Continent cannot offer this country a long-term future, except as one among many trading partners.' [17]

He further contradicts the Chancellor by revealing that Britain would suffer no economic disadvantage if it withdrew from the EU. His cost analysis of the benefits of membership has confirmed that Britain 'barely breaks even', and that if Britain ultimately came under unbearable pressure to sign up to a single currency or stringent social regulations, there are benefits to be considered in going it alone. His analysis looks at Britain's contribution to the Common Agricultural Policy (around £10 billion per annum), which is roughly off-set by the £9 billion net trade gain. He concludes:

'In the short term it makes sense to remain an EU club member, since we have invested so much in it. But if Britain's EU partners insist on signing up to the Social Chapter or joining the monetary union, the costs of the relationship would erase Britain's hard-won economic advantages.' [18]

It is not so much the facts about monetary union which need revealing in this book. They are dealt with in Bernard Connolly's informative book *The Rotten Heart of Europe*. The concern here is more with the manipulation and distortion of those facts. Even the perspicacity of Enoch Powell's observation that the ERM implies a subversion of democracy is dismissed by John Major as 'barmy' thinking in 'cloud cuckoo land'. Britain is being drawn in by the fear of being left on the periphery, and those ringing the alarm bells are propagating the myth that *this dreadful monetary union is going to happen whether we like it or not so we've just got to close our eyes, say a few prayers, brace ourselves and walk right into it.* Outright opposition to the European Monetary System (EMS) carries with it the branding of 'anti-communautaire' – a kind of heresy, blasphemy and treason all rolled into one. It is difficult (if not impossible) to gain redemption from this state, as Margaret Thatcher found, yet even John Major stated:

'A single currency is about the *politics* of Europe, it is about a *federal* Europe by the back door.' [19]

It has therefore little to do with economic benefit or political symbols of friendship and co-operation. Monetary union has to be followed in the shortest step by political union, as the recent reunification of Germany proved. A common currency for East and West Germanys came into being on 1st July 1990, and political union, as the Bundesbank consistently asserts, automatically follows if the state is to be held together. Otmar Issing, the Chief Economist of the German Central Bank, also confirmed this, saying:

> 'There is no example in history of a lasting monetary union that was not linked to one state.' [20]

Wilhelm Nolling, a Bundesbank Council Member, also put it very clearly:

> 'We should be under no illusion – the present controversy over the new European monetary order is about power, influence and the pursuit of national interests.' [21]

The Governor of the Bundesbank, Hans Tietmeyer, has made the implication crystal clear:

> 'A European currency will lead to member nations transferring their sovereignty over financial and wage policies as well as in monetary affairs ... It is an illusion to think that states can hold on to their autonomy over taxation policies.' [22]

It boils down to a 'Continental' concept of state and law overriding the 'Anglo-Saxon' concept, a movement which the *Maastricht Treaty* has embodied in law. Central banking in the UK (and the United States and other 'Anglo Saxon' nations) ensures the stability of the financial system; it is a *servant* of the market and permits effective operation. In continental Europe, however, central banks have a much more political function; they are *centres of power* and not mere 'facilitators' for private markets. There is no doubt that the European Central Bank defined by Maastricht would be the sort of beast that would need to override any 'inconvenient' oscillating electoral preferences and would, therefore, be in the controlling hands of powerful financial philosophers. Otto von Habsburg MEP has called for a totally new economic philosophy to replace traditional capitalism and socialism, and has further alluded to the inconvenience of democracy. He said:

> 'With our present, short-lived state structure, five or six-year plans are the furthest one can look ahead. In view of the size of the task – which includes the complete reconstruction of the economic order as well as of economic thought – it is clear that the narrow temporal limitations of planning periods will have deleterious effects. It must at least become possible to think and prepare for more than the span of one generation.' [23]

The differing systems of banking and the political mind-sets which exist in the diverse nations of Europe are now vying for control of the European superstate. It is a struggle particularly visible between France and Germany, with both sides claiming the heritage of the crown of Charlemagne. There was a curious symbolic expression of this struggle at the Aachen summit of 1978, when the leaders of those nations paid a special visit to the throne of Charlemagne. Afterwards, the French president, Giscard d'Estaing, remarked:

> 'Perhaps when we discussed monetary problems, the spirit of Charlemagne brooded over us.' [24]

It is yet to be decided who will actually *play* Charlemagne in the new empire, but the political leaders – particularly of France and Germany – understand that monetary economics is the instrument of political leadership, and that the wider the currency's domain, the greater the power of those who control it. German Minister of Finance, Theo Waigel, has no doubts. He said:

> 'Germany as the biggest and most powerful economic member state will be the leader, whether we like it or not.'

To some potentates, the State is rather like the Word in John's Gospel – all that is made was made by it and without it nothing was made – and there is an inherent belief in its goodness and power, a power which will always prevail over trivial issues like economics. Therefore, any nation prepared to 'go it alone' and pursue an inflation-targeting approach for its own real-world economy is choosing the surest route of reducing the political power of a central bank and retaining the accountability of monetary authorities. The Bundesbank may view Wall Street or the London Stock Exchange as casinos, but they are financial institutions which are accountable and open to regulation and scrutiny. The European oligarchy sees that it is all the more important for Britain to be a part of EMU, if the power of the European Bank is not to be undermined.

## In for a penny . . .

There are in circulation all sorts of curious justifications of the need for a common currency, but none is more absurd than the story told by the European Commissioner, Sir Leon Brittan. He cites the imaginary case of an innocent traveller who leaves the UK with £100 in his pocket to make an impromptu tour of the EU countries. He changes his pounds into francs, pesetas, lira, marks etc. as he crosses each border. Each time, he loses 2–3 per cent in tourist exchange rates. On completing this bizarre process, he returns to the UK and changes his money back into sterling without having spent a penny anywhere (a further peculiar feature of this story). He discovers, to his horror, that he has less than £50 left. Now, anyone eccentric enough to behave in this way, rather than carry a credit or cash card, might also be senseless enough to listen to Sir Leon. The minuscule percentages of tourist commission handed over by innocent travellers pale into utter insignificance beside the vast costs of EMU and the phenomenal shocks intrinsic to the process of unifying divergent economies. The percentages are also tiny compared to the vast amounts of publicly-admitted CAP fraud. For the unification process to be implemented, the productivity and income standards of each nation would need harmonising. So too would the balances between public and private sectors, government regulation and subsidy, social security systems, and education. Further, there would need to be the assurance that no member state could ever diverge from these harmonisations, a specification implying the prior existence of a single government with considerable political power, and a federal system weighted towards the centre. Again, the Habsburg vision surfaces, with Otto von Habsburg stating:

'It is not only a question of creating a new economic order ... What we have to build is a new order which will embrace the whole of life, constructed from a single, coherent point of view ... It is impossible in practice to keep the various functions of society separate. Economics, social welfare and politics are indivisible; they are but different manifestations of the same process of life.'

Certainly for France and Germany, EMU is not an economic issue but a means of shifting political power between the two countries. Monetary and political union cannot be traded off; they are different sides of the same coin: in for a penny, in for a Euro. Bernard Connolly, who headed the EC's policy unit monitoring the ERM until he exposed its corruption in his revealing book, was hardly better placed to observe and warn:

'A currency has meaning because it expresses national monetary sovereignty. The circumstances that might make a country want to give up its national monetary sovereignty irrevocably can never have anything rationally to do with economics – though the connection is often falsely made. A reason can be found only in politics or, more accurately, in the desire of certain groups to create, extend or buttress power for themselves at the expense of the electorates they are supposed to serve.'[25]

There is a sustained conditioning of the British mind (certainly by the current Chancellor, Kenneth Clarke, and his fellow pro-European shadow, Gordon Brown) that the UK is defeated and in decline and the only positive notes are Euro-optimistic ones. The tired metaphors of 'missing the bus', 'trains leaving the platform' and 'being in the slow lane' are wheeled out again and again, making a consistent preparation for the British loss of national independence and the acceptance of what is termed the 'historic inevitability'. There are, however, undeniable advantages in missing a bus which is going to crash, or driving in the slow lane when the bridge around the corner has collapsed. The hard drive by Jacques Delors to form a new super-Bundesbank at European level – totally independent of governments and consequently able to exercise a degree of power beyond the wildest dreams of many heads of government – is nothing to do with Margaret Thatcher's liberal single market. It has everything to do with keeping the poorer countries poor and shielding the wealthier ones from competitive devaluations, thus preserving their wealth.

## Bridges, windows and doors

On 13th April 1996, the EU finance ministers agreed that the sub-unit of the Euro should be named the 'Euro-cent', and on 13th December of that year, they released the designs of the Euro banknotes. It is envisaged that production of these will begin in 1998, and they will be issued for circulation shortly after the establishment of the European Central Bank, by 1st January 2002 at the latest. The banknotes will be issued in seven denominations, ranging from Euro 5 to Euro 500 (the name for the collective currency is to appear before the number).

The winning design for these banknotes is an interesting example of the importance of conveying the right image. They will all bear the EU's 12-star circle, but the main artwork will consist of drawings of bridges, windows and doors. The subliminal message is obvious. Bridges span canyons, valleys and gulfs, enabling safe passage over turbulent waters or other obstacles and dangers. Doors open to new destinations, and close on the place of origin. Their opening permits a forward move while their closing becomes a barrier to a backward step. Windows permit clear views; their transparency allows the observation of another location while being able to remain detached from the elements affecting that location. It is a wonderful example of art being used to convey a propaganda message: the bridges and doors communicate that the European Union has a clear directional objective. It is about progress and forward momentum. The windows convey the impression of clarity and openness. Had the designers been willing to represent something nearer the truth, they would have designed banknotes displaying darkened tunnels, distorting mirrors, brick walls, doorbolts and padlocks.

### References

1. Madrid conference, 15th December 1995, cited in the *New York Times*, 16th December 1995.
2. *Europe – The Crunch*, Bill Cash, The European Foundation, 1995.
3. *Maastricht Treaty*, Articles 102A, 109M and 5.
4. *Bundesbank Annual Report*, 1995.

5.  *Daily Telegraph*, 10th February 1995; *Financial Times*, 2nd December 1996.
6.  *The Times*, 18th November 1996.
7.  Quoted from *Maastricht: A Christian Dilemma*, Graham Wood, CIB.
8.  Speech to the Bruges Group, 20th February 1996.
9.  *The Business Agenda for a Free Europe*, European Research Group, London.
10. *Ibid.*
11. *Ibid.*
12. *Ibid.*
13. *Ibid.*
14. *The Times*, 12th May 1996.
15. *The Rotten Heart of Europe*, Bernard Connolly, Faber & Faber, 1995.
16. *Ibid.*
17. *The Times*, 12th May 1996.
18. *The Times*, 14th June 1996.
19. *Euromyths*, CIB, 1995.
20. *The Rotten Heart of Europe*, Bernard Connolly, Faber & Faber, 1995.
21. *Ibid.*
22. *Ibid.*
23. *The Social Order of Tomorrow*, Otto von Habsburg, Oswald Wolff Publishers, London.
24. *The Rotten Heart of Europe*, Bernard Connolly, Faber & Faber, 1995.
25. *Ibid.*

# Chapter 7

# The Real Cost

*'Thou sellest thy people for nought, and dost not increase
thy wealth by their price.'*                    (*Psalm 44:12*)

The economic case for membership of the EU is much less
obvious in the 1990s than it was in the 1970s. Tariffs
everywhere are much lower, global free trade permits
the proliferation of industrial goods, and non-European
countries like Japan and the United States have the same
access to the European single market that Britain enjoys.
For all the media hype about membership of the EU being
crucial for Britain's economic well-being, the facts are less
than conclusive. The benefits of membership cost the British
people 0.25 per cent of Gross Domestic Product (GDP) per
annum – around £9 billion. Some believe that the benefits
flowing from the EU into Britain amount to that each
year – an idea which former chancellor Norman Lamont
refuted, stating: 'Even if it did, it would hardly be the
bargain of the century.'[1] But the political costs attributed to
the inefficiency incurred by a fledgling European government make the entire machine a grossly ineffective means of
administering those benefits. Payments to the EU budget
currently exceed grants and receipts by some £4 billion
per annum, making Britain a net giver to the EU (see
Appendix 3). It will help to examine a few financial and

economic facts and compare them with the misinformation and half truths which have circulated since 1973.

## The truth, the whole truth, and something quite like the truth

Edward Heath informed the British people that membership of the EEC would have a 'positive and substantial' effect on the balance of trade. The truth of the matter is that since joining the EEC in 1973, Britain has amassed an enormous trade deficit with Europe of almost £70 billion. Fewer than half of Britain's exports go to the EU, and only a quarter of overseas investments are with the EU. Less than 5 per cent of investment in Britain is from the EU. Over this same period, Britain has achieved a trade *surplus* with the rest of the world of more than £80 billion, and 75 per cent of overseas investment continues to go outside the EU. Further, surveys indicate that the EU is industry's least favoured option for future overseas investment. Membership of the EU has nothing to do with Britain's ability to trade with the EU. Switzerland, not even associated with the European Economic Area, exported per capita in 1993 three-and-a-half times as much to the EU as Britain did. Norway exported three times as much, and Sweden twice as much (Sweden was then outside the EU).

It was further asserted that if Britain left the EU, trade would suffer and sterling would be devalued. Again, the passing of time has proved the falsehood. Just 20 years after the UK left EFTA to join the EEC, every single member of EFTA was richer than every member of the EU except Luxembourg. In 1994, Norway rejected membership of the EU. In doing so, she retained all the trading advantages which Britain has, but suffers none of the bureaucratic regulations which British industry is subject to. On receiving the news of the 'No' vote, the Norwegian stock exchange rose and inflation fell to an all-time low. Norway has also kept all her fishing grounds intact. In 1992, Switzerland rejected membership of the European Economic Area, a move which caused the Swiss franc to rise in value. Switzerland's stock market has since risen by more than 600 points. Swiss interest rates have fallen, as have inflation and unemployment. According to UN statistics, Swiss citizens are the wealthiest in Europe, followed by the peoples of Liechtenstein, Norway and Iceland – all nations outside the EU. Even the *Financial Times* was forced to concede:

> 'Switzerland these days looks like a good advertisement for staying out of the European Union.'

Clearly, Britain does not have to sacrifice its freedoms in order to enjoy prosperity. When Britain joined the EEC, it was the third richest member state and the second richest member of EFTA. Today, Britain is the fourth poorest country in the EU and poorer than all the EFTA members.

The notion that Britain needs to be 'at the heart of Europe' is historical nonsense. Britain has always been a global trading power, free to trade with its Commonwealth, with the Americas, with Asia and with Europe. The bond of European protectionism is having, and will continue to have, a damaging effect on Britain's balance of payments. One of Britain's Japanese investors states:

> 'I would argue that the world beyond Europe is every bit as important for Britain's economic interests.' [2]

Japan, incidentally, also invests heavily in Hungary, a country which is not an EU member. Britain is also the world's largest investor in the world's largest economy – the USA. Britain receives almost twice as much inward investment from the Commonwealth as from the EU. The truth is that Britain is at the heart of the world. Being 'at the heart of Europe', a phrase used by the openly federalist European People's Party, can do little to change the direction of the EU to suit Britain's agenda.

Some economists and politicians assert that being in the EU disciplines Britain to control public expenditure and monetary policy. But the true cost of membership of the EU is rarely placed before the people – and the facts here are alarming. The British taxpayers' gross contribution to the EU is the equivalent of 5.4p on the basic rate of income tax (1996/7 rates). Withdrawal from the EU would permit a substantial cut in the rate of income tax, and the cost of living would fall further by withdrawal from the Common Agricultural Policy (on which the EU spends more than half its money). This European protection policy inflates the cost of many basic foodstuffs to 150 per cent above world market prices. It operates by price-fixing, manipulating market supply, and practices such as paying farmers to keep their fields fallow.

> *'Unused fields could yield plenty of food for the poor, but unjust men keep them from being farmed.'*
> (*Proverbs 13:23* GNB)

The Organisation for Economic Co-operation and Development (OECD) says the CAP increases the average British family's food bill by £18 every week – almost £1000 per year. The vastness of this concealed tax outweighs any supposed benefits of 'discipline' exerted by the EU on Britain. On 20th October 1995, *The Times* reported figures worked out by researchers in the House of Commons library. They said that a pint of milk costing 36p would be 17p without the cost of supporting the CAP. A kilogram of sugar at 71p would be more than halved to 33p, and a large sliced loaf of bread costing 53p would cost just 38p. The price of beefsteak and mince is also more than doubled. Lamb increases by more than a third, and chicken and pork by about a quarter. Stephen Byers MP, who asked the Commons library to work out the figures, observed:

> 'For the first time we can see in pounds and pence the price being paid by consumers because of the CAP.'

In addition to this, fraud and lax management cost EU taxpayers up to £2 billion in 1994, according to figures produced by the EU's own Court of Auditors.

## Money, money, money...

While the lie that a single currency is necessary for a single market is widespread throughout Europe, one only needs to look at the single market shared by the US, Mexico and Canada to see that it is possible for such a market to function perfectly well without a shared currency. Viewed in this light, monetary union becomes more of a political exploit than an economic necessity. As has already been mentioned, all of the Bank of England's reserves would be handed over to the European Central Bank in Germany, and all of Britain's foreign exchange earnings (£79 billion per annum) would be transferred to benefit the Euro-state and its single currency. Already, the British Government is no longer free to raise and repeal taxes because of Article 99 of the *Maastricht Treaty*, which states:

> 'The Council shall, acting unanimously on a proposal from the Commission and after consulting with the European Parliament and the Economic and Social Committee, adopt provisions for the harmonisation of legislation concerning turnover taxes, excise duties and other forms of indirect taxation to the extent that such harmonisation is necessary to ensure the establishment and the functioning of the internal market within the time limit laid down in Article 7a.'

## VAT's the way to do it

VAT, which Britain was obliged to introduce in 1973, is the compulsory element of the tax system of EU member states. The VAT imposed on domestic fuel and power was a part of that harmonisation process and, while rates of VAT may vary, no British government is now able to repeal the tax. This was confirmed by the Shadow Chancellor, Gordon Brown MP, when interviewed on the *Today* programme. He said:

> 'I would prefer it to be removed altogether, but it can't be done.'[3]

Here is a prospective Chancellor of the Exchequer who wishes to repeal a Conservative tax admitting that *it can't be done*. Brussels decrees that once VAT has been imposed on any product, it cannot be subsequently zero-rated. Britain's exemptions (food, children's clothing, books, newspapers, public transport, house purchases) are all subject to challenge and Europe-wide harmonisation (see Appendix 2). Any British government which promises that the VAT net will not widen denies the reality of a legally binding treaty and in so doing deceives the British electorate. Commission President Jacques Santer told the European Parliament that VAT harmonisation is a priority, and that he is going to make full use of the legalities of Maastricht.

VAT is the most obvious of all European taxes because it reaches into everyday spending. More concerning are the concealed means of raising revenue. It is estimated that around a million British jobs have been destroyed since 1973 through the CAP, and because of the imposition of the EU's external tariff wall, which has distorted British trade. Even the leader of the Labour Party, Tony Blair, expressed this view in 1983, saying:

> 'We'll negotiate a withdrawal from the EEC, which has drained our natural resources and destroyed jobs.'[4]

Professor Patrick Minford wrote in *The European Journal* in November 1995:

> 'The idea that a single currency would reduce unemployment is fanciful in the extreme. First, to qualify for EMU, all states must cut their government deficits below 3 per cent of GDP and their public debt below 60 per cent of GDP. Yet nearly all EU countries are way over these limits – this implies large cuts in public expenditure or, more likely given difficulties in such cuts, rises in taxation – hardly a recipe for growth and job creation. The greatest likelihood is that the stringent Maastricht criteria will be somehow relaxed, permitting the political process of monetary union to proceed with little regard for the economic consequences. Secondly, a single currency removes a state's ability to reduce its interest rates below that set by the Central Bank and, of course, to move its exchange rate. This will certainly deepen recessions when they occur. Some countries, facing severe lack of competitiveness and prevented from interest rate cuts and devaluation, may face prolonged unemployment to force down wages.'

This is a moral issue, since such policies *'trample on the heads of the poor ... and deny justice to the oppressed'* (*Amos 2:7*). On average, Britain has paid an annual net contribution of £3 billion to the EU – a sum equivalent to the total annual capital spending on NHS hospitals and equipment. This increased to £4.1 billion in 1995. Gross payments to Brussels are currently running at £197 million per week – enough to give every one of our nine million pensioners an extra £20 each week. This is a moral issue, since Scripture clearly condemns those *'who oppress the poor and crush the needy'* (*Amos 4:1*). Between 1973 and 1991, Britain has lost to Brussels the net sum of £25 billion – enough, according to one estimate, to rebuild the entire Intercity rail network.

If all the costs to Britain of EU membership were added up – the costs of the CAP, the accumulated trade deficit, net contributions to the European budget, and the cost to British industry of complying with EU regulations – the total figure would reach £235 billion. That is equivalent to £4000 for every man, woman and child in Britain.

Future costs would certainly include, according to Jacques Delors, the vast black hole of European unfunded pension debt. Even despite Britain's prudent policy of funding future pensions by way of contributions and investments during the pensioner's working life, there is still an accumulated deficit for Britain of some £250 billion claimable by civil servants and NHS employees. The total EU pension debt, of which 99.7 per cent has been incurred on the Continent, has reached the stupefying total of £10,000,000,000,000,000 (£10 trillion). British taxpayers of the future will consequently have to pay billions of pounds either in additional taxation or high interest rates. David Shaw MP has calculated that every new-born British baby would arrive with a £39,000 'birth duty'.[5] Those in power would do well to ponder such a prospect:

> *'Woe to those ... who defraud a man of his home, a fellow man of his inheritance.'*     (*Micah 2:2*)

## References

1. *The Times*, 12th May 1996.
2. Haruko Fukuda, Vice-Chairman of Nikko Securities.
3. *Today* programme, BBC Radio 4, 30th October 1996.
4. *Sunday Telegraph*, 1st October 1995.
5. *Hansard*, House of Commons speech, 7th June 1996.

# Chapter 8

## War or Peace?

*'For we wrestle not against flesh and blood, but against principalities, against powers, against the rulers of the darkness of this world, against spiritual wickedness in high places.'*

(*Ephesians 6:12*)

Certain geographical areas and towns have had prominent roles throughout European history. The fields around Brussels, the current nerve centre for the creation of the European State, are where the Napoleonic European Empire was brought to an end, and this is also the area where British soldiers fired their first shots 50 years later at the outbreak of the First World War. Maastricht, where the treaty was signed which dissolved British sovereignty, undermined the British throne and established European citizenship, is the home of a shrine to Mary. It has, since 1400, been at the centre of Dutch religious struggles between Roman Catholics and Reformers. It is the town where the Gunpowder Plot was hatched by a group of Roman Catholics, who attempted to destroy the Protestant throne of James I. Interestingly, in 1550, there also originated in Maastricht a pageant in which the central figure was a giant with two figures in his pouch – a bishop and a king. A Dutch pamphlet explains that the Maastricht merchants were opposed to the centralising regime of the Habsburg

Emperor Charles V, and invented the savage giant to symbolise the fact that the financial leaders of the city had the Bishop of Liege and the Emperor Charles in their sack. The Maastricht message was straightforward: economic forces are more powerful than Church or State; Mammon overrules both spiritual and political principles. Considering that the *Maastricht Treaty* of 1992 was the treaty by which the European single currency became the driving force of European integration, the spiritual ruling powers of Maastricht seem to be stirring once again.

Dunkirk, prior to the Second World War, was famous for the Battle of Dunes in 1658, where Admiral Blake put a stop to Spanish ascendancy. Since that time, Britain has played a leading role in the shaping of Europe. For example, it organised the coalition to curb French dominance under Louis XIV, helped to draw up the *Treaty of Utrecht* which settled the pattern of Europe for the 18th century, and organised the coalition against Napoleon. Britain also took a leading role in formulating the *Treaty of Vienna* (which settled the pattern of Europe for the 19th century), the *Treaty of Versailles* (which set the national boundaries that still exist today), and it helped to conclude the settlement following the Second World War. Though some of these treaties may have been flawed, Britain has consistently taken a crucial lead in defending freedom and democracy, and has since assisted the British Colonies and other nations in drawing up their constitutions to become independent states. Britain's past is not without shame, but in the recent fighting for peace against the forces of pride, prejudice and greed, there has been a dedication to Christian principles and a wholehearted commitment to destroying oppressive political and religious systems.

It is difficult to understand the past existence of three German Reichs, and a concerted drive for a fourth, without entertaining the notion of territorial principalities and powers in the heavenly realm. To dismiss this notion altogether would imply that the recurrent Maastricht appearances, and Germany's recurring dominance, were simply coincidental. The Bible is clear that there is no rest for Christians from the battles against the spiritual principalities and powers which oppose the purposes of God. The king of adversaries, Satan, governs demon princes who have dominion over specified geographical areas. A principality is precisely that – an area governed by a prince. In *Daniel 10* there is mention of the prince of Persia, and a little later the prince of Greece. *Ezekiel 27* talks about the ruler of Tyre, who seems to reflect the attributes of Satan himself, and one of God's archangels, Michael, is called the Prince of Israel (*Daniel 12:1*). It is possible that Satan has his trusted princes over all the governments of this world. These princes are responsible to him for carrying out his will in those governments. He seeks to hinder God's plan in the fulfilment of prophecy regarding world kingdoms.

Since Michael is named as the Prince of Israel, it is clear that God also has trusted angels to carry out His will concerning what He has ordained for the kingdoms of this world, and these opposing forces are even now locked in an immense war in the heavenlies. On this basis, all wars lost or won on earth are congruous with wars which are lost or won by these heavenly armies. The political is only a product of the spiritual. It is God who plans the rise and fall of kingdoms, and Satan who seeks to confound those plans. Such demon princes may also influence national characteristics. These could be examined globally, but the principal concern here is Europe. The evidence of history indicates massive heavenly battles, with adversarial races like the Frankish or Germanic peoples vying for European supremacy, and nations like Britain, who in recent history at least, warring to defend liberty, democracy and justice. It is also noteworthy that nations like Switzerland, which previously opted for neutrality in times of war, have adopted a peripheral neutrality on the EU.

## The bombs of peace

The politics of the next few years will determine whether Europe is about to enter a period of progress or of chaos – terms which have interchangeable interpretations depending on the individual's Euro-perspective. Ever since the Reformation, with the establishment of the Church of England and the constitutional rule of law based on biblical Protestantism, the principalities and powers of Europe have warred against Britain many times in order to effect a subjugation and a return to the Roman Catholic fold. Had Britain ever been defeated, the European Union would now be a very different continent. Yet for all the historic British defence of God-given liberties and blessings, the nation is now being defeated by a new war; not the traditional sort of conflict where millions of soldiers are shot, civilians maimed, cities bombed or nations brought to their knees in humiliating surrender to the victor, but the most ingenious form of warfare ever devised – a disabling peace. This master strategy is achieving what centuries of bloodshed have failed to win – a Britain conquered by a European oppressor. When the actions of a conqueror are examined, it is clear that they differ little from the actions of the EU government over Britain:

1. The nation's flag is lowered and the conqueror's is raised. This symbolically asserts the supremacy of the new ruling authority. A flag affirms nationhood; it informs citizens of where they came from and where they belong. The EU flag now adorns many buildings of national importance, especially on the newly instituted 'Europe Day' – an annual celebration of the Europe ideal. During many events spotlit by huge media interest – such as Euro '96 – the EU flag either replaces the Union Jack or is flown equal with it. While some assert that the use of the Union Jack on the proposed British identity cards would offend Irish nationalists – and call

for its removal – British nationalists have no say about the European symbol, which has to appear on any proposed ID cards by European directive.

2.  The national anthem, another symbol of a nation state, is replaced by an anthem whose music and lyrics reflect the heritage and aspirations of the conqueror. The EU anthem – the 'Ode to Joy' from Beethoven's ninth symphony – is, of course, German. As wonderful as this music may be, there is little likelihood that Beethoven himself would have approved its use for the emerging European Empire. He was utterly disgusted when Napoleon – whom he had previously revered – appointed himself Emperor, a move which caused him to angrily scratch out Napoleon's name from the dedication of his third symphony. The lyrics, which are by another German, Schiller, describe the entering of the shrine of a pagan goddess, and the uniting of all men as brothers by magical power.

3.  The passport, the means of foreign travel, is either withdrawn or absorbed into the conqueror's diplomatic documentation. The blue British passport has been abolished and replaced by the red European passport, affirming citizenship of the European state.

4.  The head of state is removed, principally because that person inspires loyalty. Such power and popularity have to be diminished or destroyed for the conqueror to rule unchallenged. There is no head of state in Britain with sovereign power, given that the Queen's power is undermined by imposed European citizenship, Parliament's powers are subjugated to those of the European Commission, and British courts are overruled by European judicial powers. Otto von Habsburg favours an elected head of state for Europe – not with an hereditary succession, but elected for life. The

emergence of a new Holy Roman Emperor is immensely symbolic. Habsburg says:

> 'Now we do possess a European symbol which belongs to all nations equally. This is the Crown of the Holy Roman Empire, which embodies the tradition of Charlemagne, the ruler of a united occident ... the Crown represents not merely the sovereignty of the monarch, but also the ties between authority and the people. True, it is the monarch who is crowned, but in this sacred act he appears as the representative of the whole people. It should therefore be considered whether the European head of state, as the protector of European law and justice, should not also become the guardian of a symbol which, more than any other, represents the sovereignty of the European community.' [1]

Who might this new head of state be? Delors? Santer? Kohl? It is more likely to be the Pope. The crown of the Holy Roman Empire would appear incongruous on the head of any other.

5.　The media is controlled. Reporting of facts is manipulated to favour the conqueror and a propaganda war is waged to win the hearts and minds of the people. Opinions openly expressed against the conqueror are ridiculed and dismissed. This is dealt with at length in the next chapter.

6.　The constitution and culture are set aside. Laws are imposed in direct contradiction of constitutional law, and the nation's heritage and institutions are brushed away as the conqueror reforms the legislature to meet his needs. As previously observed, European law is irreconcilable with the British constitution – and therefore undermines it.

7. The education system is controlled. As the conqueror's philosophies permeate future generations, history is re-written, the truth is misrepresented and the nation's history is subsumed by the larger world vision. Educational indoctrination is also examined in the next chapter.

8. The national religion is changed. It is either abolished and replaced with a new religion or philosophy, or it is undermined and eroded by the removal of crucial foundations and the passing of new laws. With the demise of the Church of England, the neglect of the monarch's oath to uphold the 'Protestant Reformed Religion', and the strategic ascendancy of Roman Catholics to powerful media and advisory positions, Britain's national religion is already in a state of terminal decline.

9. Ownership rights are diminished. What the state requires belongs to the state, and all the nation's reserves can be claimed by the conqueror without compensation. Thus the Common Agricultural Policy and the Common Fisheries Policy bring these food reserves under Brussels control. Other European nationals can register their boats in the UK to obtain a share of the UK fish quota. Parliament tried to outlaw this in 1988 – but the legislation was declared illegal and overturned by the European Court; evidence indeed of British loss of self-government. The establishment of a Central European Bank will complete the process, absorbing all the UK's national assets, including North Sea oil and vast gold reserves. A recent concern, and one expressed by Frank Field MP, is that the £600 billion set aside for the UK's future pension liabilities will also become a shared asset. According to the OECD, Britain's forethought in planning for its pensioners is greater than that of all the other European nations combined.

10. A form of slavery may be imposed. This may not be as extreme as whips being cracked over aching backs, but financial controls or the restriction of freedoms amount to a more subtle form of slavery. As explained in Chapter 6, money is power. Those who control the interest rates become the masters of the poor – especially if they cannot be removed from power by popular vote.

11. The nation is disarmed. The military might of the vanquished is absorbed into the might of the conqueror to make armed resistance impossible. The 1996 Inter-Governmental Conference (IGC) has moved to place a common European defence force firmly on the agenda. Both France and Germany desire such a force, with army, navy and airforce under European governmental control.

Examining the details of these actions, it is not un-reasonable to assert that Britain is being diplomatically manipulated and defeated through a peaceful war. Any mention of patriotism or nationalism incurs the disdain of political, intellectual or religious élites, as though the EU guaranteed peace and harmony, and patriotism or nation-alism caused conflicts and wars. Yet the true cause of wars is human nature – especially the lust for control and power. The prophet Jeremiah spoke wisely when he said:

> '*The heart is deceitful above all things, and desperately wicked.*' (*Jeremiah 17:9*)

Human sympathy normally spreads outwards from indi-viduals to families, then to extended families and friends, and onwards to form communities, regions and countries, as people discover common ties of kinship, language and culture. God made the nations with diverse qualities, and these variations of national characteristics and cultures display a wonder of creation. If the story of the Tower of

Babel established anything, it was that segregation occurs along these lines, and that attempts to re-build a unified tower are doomed to failure. There was never meant to be a bland uniformity, and totalitarian governments which have attempted to impose such a conformity have presided over nationalistic discontent and civil wars. Free states extend the hand of peace and friendship to their neighbours in an appreciation of other cultures and nations. The love of one's own country permits an understanding of the love others have for theirs, and no amount of patriotic feeling, nationalistic zeal or blindness to national diversity can lead to war. War is the manifestation of the lust for power and domination which is found in human nature, especially the power of dictators motivated by trans-national ideologies based on race, class, religious ideals or utopianism – such as Nazism, Communism or totalitarianism. These, not nationalism, have been the great scourge of 20th century Europe, and one of the principal barriers to their advance has been the patriotic resistance of nations determined to defend their own rights, liberties and heritage.

## The diminishing veto

Despite the assurances being offered with regard to the British veto, particularly in regard to defence matters, each successive European treaty has seen an erosion of British vetos, extensions of qualified majority voting and a weakening of Britain's ability to act autonomously. On 28th February 1996, the European Commission stated:

> 'In an enlarged Union, adherence to unanimity would often result in stalemate. Indeed, the difficulty of arriving at unanimous agreements rises exponentially as the number of members increases. The Commission accordingly proposes that qualified majority voting become the general rule.'[2]

The vision was encapsulated by one MEP:

> 'We want the minority to accept what the majority has decided.'[3]

There is every reason to suspect that a common European defence union would constitute another slippery slope towards federalism, if merely because Britain is directly accountable to the European Court of Justice. Should that Court rule that Britain may not fight a war to protect its territories, Britain would be powerless. Imagine a veto-less Britain trying to defend its territory in the Falkland Islands. It would not have been possible, since some European countries opposed the war. If military divisions and regiments were pooled, Britain would find it harder to act (or withdraw) unilaterally. Some might argue that this further loss of sovereignty would be acceptable if, as a result, the spectre of war in Europe were laid to rest once and for all – but that is unlikely. A European army could be called to the Balkans, Cyprus or wherever else European tensions existed, and Britain could find itself embroiled in conflicts which it did not consider 'just'. The nations of Western Europe are all now peace-loving democracies, and this philosophy of government is being embraced by the nations of Eastern Europe. This is the principal reason for 50 years of peace in Europe. Democracy, NATO, and mutual respect are the best guarantors of peace; an erosion of any of them could create tensions and conflicts which no number of treaty obligations would quell.

## The Franco-German axis

There is a perception, borne out by some senior European officials, that the entire European agenda is adhering to a timetable which suits Germany and France. As Margaret

Thatcher observed, everyone else must simply fall into line. That the Germans invariably place their own national interest before the common good of the Union was proven by events following German reunification. Sterling was tied into a narrow ERM band, and Britain was in recession and desperately needing a cut in interest rates. Germany, however, doggedly maintained high interest rates, which eventually led to the ejection of sterling from the ERM. Germany was not concerned with Britain's problems; neither was it concerned with the European interest. Instead, its own domestic political needs became the dominating influence on the entire European economic situation. The Bundesbank is required to consider only its domestic needs; the needs of the rest of Europe are of little consequence. As the two Germanys united their currencies in 1990, it became impossible for East Germany to go on existing as a separate political entity. Monetary union precludes any aspiration to independent political identity, as Chancellor Kohl knows. The French foreign minister, Hervé de Charette, confirmed this:

'The Franco-German axis must continue to fulfil its federating function ... The single currency project is the principal and ... only European federating project ... the powerfully federalist character of this project has yet to be appreciated.'[4]

Senior European economists also affirm that decisions are partly rigged in advance by the two largest member states – Germany and France – which are bound by the terms of their bilateral treaty of 1963 to reach 'as far as possible an analogous position'[5] *ahead* of meetings of the Council of Ministers. This state of affairs makes a nonsense of John Major's refrain that Britain should be 'at the heart of Europe', since its heart is occupied by Germany and France. This may explain the constant ministerial refrain of 'fighting

Britain's corner in Europe'. Corners are not at the heart; they are at the periphery.

It was hoped that a European Union would provide a much-needed check on German domination, but the re-unification has instead spawned a giant power with a greater propensity for flexing its muscles. The battle for German unification caused numerous wars in the 19th century, and its battle for supremacy has caused the two bloodiest wars in the 20th century. Though the plan remains the same, the tactics have now changed. The aim is to bring about the peaceful union of Europe under a dominant Germany, to achieve without bloodshed what the Kaiser and Hitler failed to win on the battlefield. The danger is that this aim totally ignores the democratic process. People may be taking their liberties for granted, but the sudden loss of control over their economy may begin to wake them up. A single currency will emulate a permanent, constraining ERM, drawn up on German and French rules. As jobs and investment transfer from Britain to the Paris-Berlin axis, and the poorer parts of the EU become completely subservient to wealthier members who hold the purse-strings, one effect will certainly be a revival of nationalism. People will begin to notice that monetary and economic union is robbing them of their liberty and national identity. As undemocratic direct-ives, regulations and laws flow from Brussels, people will begin to realise that they need to regain their liberties. The hope that secession might be possible without wars for independence is diminished when one examines an ominous line of the *Maastricht Treaty*, which states:

> 'The Union shall provide itself with the means neces-sary to attain its objectives and carry through its policies.'[6]

The chairman of the Anti-Federalist League, Dr Alan Sked, said:

'This clause, which could have come straight out of Hitler's *Enabling Act*, completely nullifies the subsidiarity principle.'[7]

Those who think this observation is reactionary and alarmist might also like to note the views of the former head of the Commission's ERM unit, Bernard Connolly. He said:

'The ERM and EMU are not only inefficient but also undemocratic: a danger not only to our wealth but to our freedoms and ultimately our peace. The ERM is a mechanism for subordinating the economic welfare, democratic rights and national freedom of citizens of the European countries to the will of political and bureaucratic élites whose power lust, cynicism and delusions underlie the actions of the vast majority of those who now strive to create a European superstate.'[8]

On 16th October 1995, Chancellor Kohl demanded that everyone must concentrate on making Europe an 'irreversible process'. This was imperative, he argued, if Europe was to avoid collapse. He went on to repeat the threat he had used on earlier occasions that Europe must do as Germany says, or there will be war in the 21st century as well:

'The construction of the House of Europe remains the only real guarantee of freedom and peace in the 21st century.'[9]

In promoting Franco-German reconciliation, the European project has been a success. The signing of the *Treaty of Rome*, in 1957, was able to secure peace because the Nazi ideology which seized Germany during the 1930s had been destroyed by Hitler's defeat. However, the EU's evolution into deeper political integration and the erosion of the independence of its member states is in danger of causing a tide of popular resentment that might destroy rather than strengthen European harmony. Maastricht, with the divisive issue of monetary union at its heart, is not the natural completion of the *Treaty of Rome*; it is a manifesto for division and conflict in Europe. As a European Central Bank emerges, France will be concerned to ensure that the institution operates in French interests as well as Germany's. But if French domestic financial matters were to cause the ECB to compromise the German agenda, there is no doubt that Germany would take swift action – either against the bank, or against France. Of course, Germanic-Frankish conflicts are nothing new. Germany has instigated the bloodiest conflicts in the history of the world, and France has known multiple revolutions and wars since 1789. Both France and Germany are only recent converts to democracy and political stability. The constraints of Maastricht, rising unemployment and the realisation that democratic principles are being abandoned could well trigger further revolution and conflict. No-one is suggesting that Jacques Chirac or Helmut Kohl would threaten each other, or any of the other European nations, with annihilation, but their policies would cause economic decline, political illegitimacy and resentment among the nations of Europe – conditions in which xenophobia would be far more likely than liberal nationalism. This would ultimately lead either to a rigid totalitarian state with rigorous control over such tensions, or a fresh outbreak of war. Former defence minister Alan Clark observed:

> 'The European Commission ... is not a programmatically hostile and aggressive force, as was Nazi Germany. *But it is not benign.* And the reason for its ill-disposition towards Britain ... is of the same nature as that felt by Napoleon, by Kaiser Wilhelm, and by Adolf Hitler.' [10]

As much as all this may be dismissed as speculation, there is one blindingly obvious factor which deserves great consideration: the European plan clearly runs counter to the course of history. With the break-up of the former USSR, the Quebec bid for independence from the Canadian federation, the former Yugoslavia's descent into tribal warfare, the splitting asunder of Czechoslovakia, and even the fracturing of the United Kingdom, the evidence is overwhelming that states established by treaties are fragile entities. Further, artificially created states invariably tend to revert back to their ethnic groupings, often with horrific wars of independence in the struggles for nation-state recognition. Lord Tebbit observed:

> 'The tragedy of Yugoslavia is not a tragedy of people fighting to come together in a federal state, it is a tragedy of people who are fighting to escape from a federal state.'

Europe is not yet rid of the spectres of Nazism; Bosnia is a timely reminder that Europe still has the capacity to produce real-life visions of emaciated, broken men staring out numbly from behind the barbed wire of concentration camps. The political structures of Western Europe have kept its countries in peace and friendship for the longest period of stability in its history, yet there has arisen a great dilemma. There are those who believe that Europe is yesterday's solution to the day-before-yesterday's problems. A union that was forged to avoid war has produced a sustained peace, but the greater and more successful that peace, the more remote the possibility of war becomes, and the harder it is to find a reason for the existence of the Union. The entire experiment has produced a great paradox.

## References

1. *The Social Order of Tomorrow*, Otto von Habsburg, Oswald Wolff Publishers, London.

2. *Reinforcing Political Union and Preparing for Enlargement*, EC, 28th February 1996.

3. Hans-Gert Pottering MEP, 11th Congress of the EPP, Reuters News Service, 7th November 1995.

4. Speech to the French branch of The European Movement, Paris, 26th June 1996.

5. *International Currency Review*, Vol. 23, No. 4, Autumn 1996.

6. *Maastricht Treaty*, Title 1 Article F3.

7. Quoted in *Maastricht made Simple*, published by *The European*, 1992.

8. *Daily Mail*, 5th September 1995.

9. CDU Annual Congress, 16th October 1995.

10. *Daily Telegraph*, 9th January 1997.

# Chapter 9

## The Propaganda Offensive

*'"What is truth?" Pilate asked.'*
*(John 18:38)*

The British press and media seem to be incapable of moderation or nuance on the matter of Europe. At one extreme is the confrontational anti-Europe cry wrapped in the Union Jack, with its jingoistic vocabulary and war allusions, and at the other is a destructive ridiculing of anyone who so much as questions the European ideal, or criticises any of its institutions. Such people are deemed to live in 'cloud cuckoo land' and know nothing of the real world. The reasoning runs thus: to criticise any European institution makes you anti-European; to be anti-European makes you nationalistic; nationalism leads to war, and war is evil; conclusion – criticising Europe is evil. There are also those who worsen the situation by equating extreme expressions of nationalism with the phrase 'protecting the British interest', making it into a religious anthem, and the Union Jack or the Cross of St. George become symbolic religious emblems.

## The reign of confusion and lies

Much has been made of Chancellor Kohl's repeated lie:

> 'European integration is, in reality, a question of war and peace in the 21st century.'

He endorsed a statement by the late President Mitterand of France in 1995 that 'nationalism is war', which is a further propaganda fabrication. Preserving the nation state is an absolute prerequisite for the preservation of freedom and physical security, given the threat to both inherent in the emergence of regional and global government. Cherishing one's nation for this reason is not synonymous with nationalism, as the promoters of the European cause deceitfully maintain, but such is the influence of EU propaganda that their campaign against 'xenophobia' is intended to neutralise and marginalise those who value the nation state. The whole move to unite humanity in a New World Order, through the abolition of nation states, is mired in lies and confusion which can only have one source:

> *'The Devil himself, which is the author of confusion and lies.'* [1]

There is a *fin de siècle* malaise which is destabilising the psyche of the British people. The European agenda, with all the associated evasion and duplicity, has permeated through all the British institutions of government. The people have become used to the lies, 'sleaze', misinformation or disinformation which now emanate from Westminster, and some sections of the media have been looking to Europe as a better example. Many people feel, either subconsciously or knowingly, nothing but contempt for their political leaders.

The difference between misinformation and disinformation is sometimes not understood. Misinformation is a pack of lies which is disseminated in error, or because of ignorance of the true facts. Disinformation is a pack of lies which the perpetrator knows to be lies, and which are disseminated deliberately. Examples of both are pervasive in the entire debate on Britain's relationship with the EU.

# Blessed are those who believe in the status quo

To pour scorn over anyone who argues for withdrawal from the European Union or in favour of a referendum on deeper integration is to contribute nothing to an important and necessary debate. Conversely, all who would promote European integration also have a right to be heard without public ridicule from the anti-European press. Britain is, after all, still essentially a democracy which enshrines the principles of free speech. Yet somehow, the truth is distorted; somehow the media fails to report the facts; somehow the very tone of enquiry undermines the presentation of the truth, and what would normally be seen as a lie or deception insidiously becomes a pseudo-truth. For instance, Otto von Habsburg states with patronising arrogance:

> 'The necessity for a unification of Europe is obvious to any thinking person.'

He seems to call into question the mental faculties of those who do not hold to such a necessity. But while John Major uses the phrase 'living in cloud cuckoo land' to denigrate Euro-opponents, David Smith, writing in the *Sunday Times*, discovered that Aristophanes created the land as a surprisingly rational place. Political scientist and philosopher Leonard Schapiro observed:

> 'The true object of propaganda is neither to convince nor even persuade, but to produce a uniform pattern of public utterance in which the first trace of unorthodox thought reveals itself as a jarring dissonance.'

This is certainly applicable to the European debate, and even more applicable to those who voice concerns about the ecumenical process between the Church of England and Rome. Anything that questions the status quo on such issues has great difficulty finding a platform or publisher. The power of the media is immense. It comes as no surprise therefore to learn that European federalists are seeking control of vast sections of it. The European People's Party states:

> 'What is at stake here is the future of European unity, so the European Community must play its full part in the reorganisation of the media. We now advocate a European television channel operating to the design of the European Broadcasting Union.'[2]

## The power of the press

It is interesting to examine the vast shift in press opinion on Europe since entry to the EEC in 1973. During the referendum campaign of 1975, the press marginalised all of Tony Benn's coherent arguments on sovereignty, and all of Enoch Powell's on culture. Each national newspaper laid aside their old rivalries in the bid to extract a 'Yes' vote from the people. Their victory boast 'We are all Europeans now!' is now the opposite – a cry of doom. In 1975, the *Daily Express* derided Tony Benn for running an 'ignoble campaign'. In 1996, he is one of their 'leading commentators'. This may be due to more than the fact that the scales are falling off the eyes of the press as they realise that British sovereignty actually *is* at stake. They are now realising that the very power base of the press itself is threatened by greater European integration. Sir Peregrine Worsthorne, writing in the *Sunday Telegraph*, observed:

> 'Twenty years ago, when the process began, there was no question of losing sovereignty. That was a lie, or at any rate, a dishonest obfuscation.'[3]

All newspapers are essentially nationalist enterprises since they aim at nationals confined within their particular borders. If political and economic decisions were further transferred from Westminster to Brussels, the press would lose its principal punchbag and would be left with trivia, not to mention substantially weakened muscles. The very raison d'être of the tabloids is their ability to sway public opinion and shape institutions – if that were removed then readership would certainly decline, if not vanish. Because of this, xenophobia and a particular anti-French and German flavour have come to dominate tabloid headlines, and there is no doubt that the British public is decidedly more anti-European than in 1975. The wheel has come full circle, and the middle ground has been swamped by the extremities of opinion. There is nothing new under the sun.

A principal example demonstrating the distortion of truth was research carried out by journalist Christopher Booker into figures from a Confederation of British Industry (CBI) survey which were quoted in Parliament. It was claimed that 71 per cent of firms were enjoying greater trading opportunities with Europe due to the single market,[4] but Booker's critique revealed quite a different story. Out of 8000 companies sent the questionnaire, only 579 responded – some 7 per cent. Of this 7 per cent, it was claimed that 71 per cent – some 411 – were benefiting directly from the single market. Actually, in the detailed questioning, only 27 per cent attributed their greater trading opportunities to the single market – some 156. The real truth here is that just under 2 per cent of British firms enjoy greater trading with the EU as a result of the single market. Similarly, much was made of the quoted 'fact' that 79 per cent of firms are actively seeking greater trading opportunities with the rest of the EU. But when asked about their attempts to seek greater trading opportunities outside the EU, almost exactly the same number of respondents gave the same answer – obviously they were simply trying to expand their trade! European Commissioner Sir Leon Brittan quoted another CBI survey, saying: 'a majority of CBI members are in favour of economic and monetary union.' In fact, fewer than a third of companies bothered to reply, and of this third (some 206 companies) only 28 per cent – fewer than 60! – responded positively to the formation of a single currency. Booker commented:

> 'It is a tribute to the power of the press release that the views of fewer than 60 firms can be solemnly reported as those of 84 per cent of CBI members.' [5]

The exposure of the CBI spin-doctors and the British Management Data Foundation's laudable revealing of truth have done nothing to persuade the more respected media organisations of the need to scrutinise misleading press releases. The BBC and four major daily broadsheets, in reporting details of the 1995 CBI survey, stated, again, that a majority of British firms favoured a single currency. Closer examination of the detailed questioning revealed that only 8 per cent of respondents – some 135 companies – agreed with the statement: 'Joining a single currency is essential to ensure British competitiveness.' This is just 135 out of a CBI membership of more than 8000 and, once again, represents under 2 per cent. There seems a marked bias of reporting and a proven inclination to ignore surveys which are judged to be inconvenient to the process of closer European integration.

The media's omission of inconvenient information has been highlighted recently by the European ban on British beef, which has focused considerable attention on the loss of sovereignty to Brussels. The Federation of Veterinarians in Europe maintains that thousands of cases of BSE have gone unreported in Europe, confirming statistics given previously by a group of scientists. Their conclusions were based on the fact that the same contaminated feed was being used across the Continent, and that livestock has been extensively exported from Britain to other EU countries. One expert believes that France ought to be reporting 200 cases a year instead of 22. It is also puzzling that the media in Holland, Luxembourg and Belgium, which between them have imported thousands of tons of contaminated feed, report no cases at all. British vets believe that Portugal should top the 'at risk' list as it imported 12,000 head of cattle, but it has only publicly reported seven cases of BSE. Spain, which might be expected to follow closely behind, has reported no cases. It is widely believed that because financial compensation is not forthcoming, cattle deaths on the Continent have been reported as due to other causes. British beef has thus been the target of a politically motivated global ban.

While it is important to recognise that this whole saga is a clear example of the consequences of perverting God's creation, by feeding meat and bonemeal to herbivorous creatures, it is also true that the EU has inflicted an unremitting propaganda campaign in continental countries against British beef alone. If the ban here is justified (as it may be), it ought to apply to other countries as well. The true facts need to emerge through the 'anti-British' rhetoric.

## Loans, grants or bribes?

The vast amount of public money spent by the European institutions on propaganda has been one of the more sinister aspects of the EU machine. The Commission's propaganda budget amounts to about £80 million for 1996, which must be added to the £120 million cost of 'information services' provided by the various departments of the Commission. The total expenditure by the Commission on propaganda and so-called 'information' is budgeted to reach about £200 million for 1996.

Information services were first defined by the leading Eurocrat, Max Kohnstamm. In a confidential memorandum dated 10th June 1954, he said their purpose was 'to disarm opponents of integration.' Next, a Franco-German public relations company, Brose and Elvinger, was appointed. In recommendations dated April 1955, the writers concluded:

> 'It is necessary to play on sentiments and to appeal ... to everything which constitutes the temperament of the crowd.'

Ever since the inception of the European Community, vast financial resources have been committed to the manipulation of 'the crowd'. More than £20 billion of taxpayers' money in net budget contributions has helped to finance the EU propaganda campaign in Britain. Though much of this may be too subtle to be detected, the British Government is openly happy to give grants to the pro-Euro-federalist 'European Movement' because it is a 'cross-party organisation'. No such finance has been granted to any anti-European 'cross-party organisation'.

A 'substantial' grant made by Baroness Thatcher to Bill Cash's European Foundation carried with it her understanding of the situation. She said:

> 'It is well known that the advocates of European federalism have never lacked access to funding. Not so those who seek to preserve British sovereignty.'[6]

The taxpayers of Britain have funded all manner of bribes offered by Commission presidents to other nations to secure pro-federalist support. Bernard Connolly observed:

'On 9th November 1991, the Irish, Spanish, Portuguese and Greek foreign ministers had left a secret meeting with Jacques Delors in which he had promised fabulous amounts (6 billion ECUs to Ireland) of other people's money if they pledged to support his federalist, corporatist ambitions in the final Maastricht negotiations. The Irish government had sold the country's soul to Delors.'[7]

Such bribes manifest themselves on hoardings all over the Union. The European flag symbol, denoting projects which have been 'funded' by the EU, is the most pervasive and innocuous means of propaganda, but it is a deception nonetheless. 'Funded' would be better described as 'loaned'. Any grants that are made to Britain have in fact been paid for by the British people, for Britain is a net contributor to the EU. An additional 50 per cent has also been wasted on EU bureaucracy. Despite this, the media continues to crow over the generosity of European grants into Britain's society.

Another example of media hype occurred on 2nd August 1996, when 'Europe' made a cash injection of £40 million into Britain's inner cities. The papers said jobs had been 'created by Europe', but of course the funds came from British taxpayers, cleverly bestowed by the EU instead of by Britain's elected Government. When one Northern Ireland project 'funded' by the EU failed to display the Euro-flag, the company was informed that they would stand a better chance of future assistance only if they displayed the Euro-flag. To use taxpayers' money to finance government propaganda agendas is scandalous but endemic. After the Danes produced a 'wrong' result in their referendum on Maastricht, their government offered them a straightforward bribe – large-scale tax cuts in return for a 'Yes' vote in the second referendum. In order to achieve the treaty's ratification, the Danish government submitted a series of opt-outs to the electorate, including clauses on the single currency, citizenship of the Union, immigration and defence. The propaganda machine warned of all the dire consequences of rejecting Maastricht a second time. Yet even as this national government assured its sovereign people of the legitimacy of these opt-outs, Chancellor Kohl was pointing out with his usual bluntness that such opt-outs had no legal standing.[8] A few thousand Danish votes could not be permitted to halt the 'march of history' or frustrate the 'general will', as decided by the key politicians of the leading EU member states. The Danes are still awaiting judgement from their Constitutional Court as to the legitimacy of the *Maastricht Treaty*. If it is ruled to be illegal there, its ratification in every other member state would collapse.

Jacques Delors was equally blunt in his abuse of any opponents of Maastricht within France, displaying a complete contempt for democracy by declaring:

> 'There is no place in a democracy for people who call for a *"Non"*, for the sorcerer's apprentices, for those who awake phantoms. I will say to them they should get out of politics.'[9]

Presumably, following the arrogant logic of the Delorsian divine will, the ordinary man in the street should get out of the country. Sadly, this arrogant manner of 'lording it over' mere citizens is endemic in all the member states, and emanates from the hearts of many politicians, bureaucrats, big businessmen, lawyers and journalists – those with power and positions of influence.

Similar tactics are to be seen again and again. For example, Brussels used taxpayers' money to persuade the Swedes to vote in favour of joining the Union. This was achieved, with a vote of 52 per cent in favour and 48 per cent against. The EU funding enabled a spending of 20 times the amount that the 'No' campaign could afford.

Along with jubilations over the enlargement of the Union to 15 nations, the press and other media promoted the benefits Sweden would now enjoy over its neighbour, Norway. But despite the pro-European media telling voters that a 'No' vote would lead to trade decline and a devalued currency, because such countries would be 'too small to survive', and despite the propagation of the myth that only a 'Yes' vote could provide stability and security of employment, the reality has been different. Even the British 'respectable' media has been remarkably reluctant to comment on the aftermath. When such facts are reported, the sheer vehemence of pro-Euro propaganda rarely permits the truth to emerge by the rational examination of the issues. The propaganda steamroller has to flatten any rational analysis because it tends to lead to dissent, and dissent will find no tolerance in the Euro-beast.

## Education and the indoctrination of children

A committee of experts chaired by the former Belgian minister and European Commissioner, Willy de Clercq, recently advocated targeting young people, deeming it 'strategically judicious to act where resistance is weakest.' The propaganda offensive is making a priority target of society's most vulnerable hearts and minds, using pamphlets, magazines and booklets aimed at school children as young as five years old. One of the most insidious is a colouring book called *Let's Draw Europe Together*, whose introduction makes its purpose clear:

> 'The title *Let's Draw Europe Together* is intended as a call to school children as well as all of us to commit ourselves to achieving European unity.'

Part One bears the slogan 'My Country: Europe', and teaches children the 'important dates' in the evolution of the EU as they colour in maps of the nations. The book goes on to explain why the EU exists:

> 'The pioneers who worked to build Europe lived through the disastrous experience of the Second World War, with all its devastation, violence and hate. Europe needed to rebuild on the basis of peace, security, understanding and solidarity. To do this, a joint body which was called the European Economic Community was needed ... The original idea of a common market has now been developed and extended into plans for a Citizen's Europe.'

On the bottom of the page is a picture of an infant carrying a large EU banner and wearing a nappy emblazoned with the 12 stars of the EU flag. In further chapters, children are introduced to the many languages of the EU and are encouraged to translate a phrase into ten languages. There is, of course, nothing wrong in introducing 5–11-year-olds to foreign languages, but the phrase they are asked to translate is the subtly indoctrinating 'Europe, our future', while their attention is kept by colouring cartoon characters.

This publication goes on to describe what the EU does, with an agriculture section expounding the Union's improvements and benefits, but telling nothing of the wastefulness and chaos of the CAP. Indeed, readers are completely misinformed about the effects of the CAP on food prices, and are told:

> 'One of the first things the EEC did was to ensure the supply of foodstuffs to European consumers at reasonable prices.'

There are many such misleading statements and pictures in this publication, which culminate in the illustration of a young man kicking down a national frontier sign and erecting in its place a large EU flag. And all this indoctrination is being funded by European taxpayers!

Another EU propaganda leaflet introduces older children to the reasons behind monetary union. It states:

'At the moment, all the countries in the European Union have different coins and notes to pay for things, but in the future we have decided to work towards having only one type of money. This would mean that when you go on holiday in another country, you would not need to go to the bank to change your money.'

Considering that the UK has secured an opt-out from any future single European currency (which receives no mention in the booklet), and that the whole subject of monetary union is hugely controversial, it is alarming that literature of this nature is circulating at all. The GCSE level publication *Europe Today* is a revealing account of a history completely at odds with the facts presented to Parliament in 1973. Consider this:

'Monnet and Schuman (the architects of the Community) were quite clear that, if it worked, their limited proposal would be the seed from which further political integration of Europe would grow.'

It makes it quite clear that the 'overall objective' of the Community was the establishment of a 'Joint Bank', confirming what Edward Heath knew all along – but kept hidden from the British electorate. Schuman, incidentally, is now on the road to beatification (the first step to 'sainthood') with the backing of the Pope.

At university level, the Commission has established European Documentation Centres and Eurodesks to offer information to 'teachers, lecturers and youth workers on the EU and the education, training and youth policies and programmes of the European Commission.' The official EU report explains the purpose of information:

> 'It is one of the instruments for citizens to think along European lines ... to shape public opinion because the general public ... is not yet sufficiently committed to the European ideal.'

The Euro-propaganda budget is vast, and dwarfs any amount raised by the anti-federalists. No budget should be used to finance propaganda, but while money is spent in this way, it is unfortunately down to teachers and parents to ensure that a balanced argument is put before the nation's children and youth.

## 'Love the Euro' campaign

On 23rd January 1996, it was announced in *The Times* that the EU intends to spend £15 million on a campaign to accustom European citizens to the idea of a single currency. The possibility of a 'Love the Euro' campaign was researched by the *European* newspaper, and various public relations companies were asked what strategy they might employ. Tom McNally of Shandwick Public Relations Agency stated how, in the event of a referendum, the Euro might be sold to the British Electorate. He declared:

> 'The first targets would have to be the business community and the city of London. They will have to be persuaded that Britain's trade and, even more importantly, London's role as Europe's financial capital would be fatally undermined if we stay outside the Euro ... A more general campaign would focus on the young ... We would recommend a Euro campaign with school competitions, conferences, magazines, and sporting and pop events. We would also tie the strength

of the Euro behind the single-issue pressure groups. Our wrap-around theme would be "The Strength of the Euro", which would be reflected in a multiplicity of campaign themes: "Put the strength of the Euro behind your children's future", "Put the strength of the Euro behind British exports", "Put the strength of the Euro behind British jobs". In the end, we would face the British people with the choice of being part of something strong and successful, or saying: "Stop the world, we want to get off".' [10]

With such a prospect, Christopher Gill MP responds:

'We do not yet know whether Britain will be granted a referendum on this issue. However, I am sure that we should feel grateful to Mr McNally for informing us of the possible ploys of the integrationists.' [11]

These tactics are nothing new. Alan Clark also warns of the manipulation process which will be used to erode Britain, and he explains why. He says:

'The British are, by nature and historically, bloody-minded and un-European. They stand in the way of "progress". They cannot be bought, as have the Greeks and the Irish; nor can they be intimidated as were the Danes after voting "No" in their first referendum. The option of humiliating them by force of arms is not (at present) realistic. So the technique for their subjection has to be gradual: to first isolate and then erode those various indicators of British national identity and self-confidence – in particular, the pillars of their constitution and the powers and status of their elected Parliament, until the point is reached when (there being so little remaining) "resistance" can be dismissed simply as nothing more than nostalgia or eccentricity.' [12]

# Propaganda tidalwaves

Some EU publications are produced to coincide with problematic situations, and such was the case with *One Market, One Money* – supposedly a research study on the alleged necessity of a monetary union. The publication of this propaganda tome, wholly anti-scientific in content, was brought forward to coincide with Margaret Thatcher's visit to Rome in October 1990; a visit which was to lead to her downfall.

She had signed the *Single European Act*, supposing it to offer improvements to free trade, but as subsequent events unfolded, she looked upon it and saw that it was not good. She began a crusade to undermine European ambitions for a new government, and publicly argued against the concept of a single European flock under one shepherd. She was losing the propaganda war back home, and some of the powers in Europe perceived their opportunity to rid the Union altogether of her swinging handbag style and opposition to monetary union. The arguments contained within *One Market, One Money* were to undermine her irreparably back home. Many of the tabloids might have been on her side, along with their readers, but the broadsheets – read by Tory MPs – were increasingly against her, siding with Nigel Lawson and the official Foreign Office view of Europe. Bernard Connolly observed:

'It became clear something was in the air when orders were given within the Commission that at all costs the publication of *One Market, One Money*, programmed for just before the December Council, must be advanced: it should now appear before the October Council. *One Market, One Money* was a piece of blatant neo-functionalist propaganda, a set of specious anti-economic arguments and rigged model simulation results intended to give support to the idea that the

Single Market in the Community required a single currency if it was to work properly. The document was long, heavy, deliberately technical and abstruse, in order both to mask its twisted logic and to impress "opinion-formers" with its "scientific" authority. The economics of this publication were immediately demolished by Professor Patrick Minford, but it achieved its aims – at least in the short term, which was what mattered politically – with dismaying completeness.' [13]

Though such devious scheming may sound unacceptably Shakespearean in character, the reality of the plot to unseat Margaret Thatcher was corroborated by a publication sent to the offices of Intercessors for Britain in 1989, reporting the activities of the Bilderbergers, a group of industrialists, bankers and world politicians. A clandestine meeting in May of that year emphasised the need to bring down Mrs Thatcher because of 'her refusal to yield British sovereignty to the European superstate that is to emerge in 1992.' It was in the autumn of that year that the first attempt to remove her was made, and within 18 months she was gone.

## The Roman road to EUtopia

The propaganda war is being fought on many fronts, but the most successful strategy is being deployed against the nation's Christian heritage. A system of government based on a throne which is Protestant by law seems to invite charges of bigotry, out-datedness and political incorrectness. The *Catholic Herald* has dismissed the work of the Protestant Truth Society as out-of-date and seen by the present generation as irrelevant in output, and preoccupied with Victorian conspiracies and plots – despite the fact that such plots have proven real, time and again. It may not be surprising that the Roman Catholic-dominated press and other media are waging a propaganda war, but the consequent ascendancy of Roman Catholicism in public esteem and respectability causes concern. Protestantism, meanwhile, is being marginalised and dismissed. The excesses of sectarian violence in Northern Ireland under the banner of Protestantism have done much to damage its meaning, so much so that few Christians would openly call themselves Protestant for fear of guilt by association. The demeaning of the name, the drives for unity in the ecumenical movement, and the search for compromise and peace have effectively rendered it politically incorrect to be known as a Protestant. The actual meaning of the word is, significantly, 'one who is for the covenant'. This is a supremely important point for those who think Protestantism is only about protesting against the errors of Romanism. The Protestant/pro-covenant truth is the foundation of the British Constitution and social fabric. Rome is still waging the war against it which began with the Counter-Reformation. Considering there are only five million Roman Catholics in Britain, with fewer than a million regular church-goers, the high media profile of the Roman Church is utterly disproportionate.

The Pope still ascribes to himself the same political and religious functions that permitted Leo III to bestow whatever earthly kingdoms he wished to Charlemagne. In a media permeated by influential Roman Catholics, little is mentioned of the Papacy's claim to sovereignty over all the world's Christians (Roman Catholics or not), or of his claim to sovereignty over all nations and all world leaders. He is still the 'Father of Kings and Princes, the Vicar of Christ and Ruler of the World', yet the media never ridicules these extravagant claims, nor even so much as questions them. How widely reported is the fact that *The Pontifical* – the service book used by the Vatican for the crowning of popes – refers to each pontiff as 'our Lord God, the Pope'? Sir Fred Catherwood may talk of the 'irrational anti-European propaganda' (as though questioning the evolving European State could never be rational), but he never once questions these absurd papal claims. The policy is one of silence in the name of ecumenical peace and harmony. Cardinal Basil Hume claimed the Roman Church 'possesses all of God's revealed truth and all the means of grace and will not accord that status on others', and there is no questioning the rationality of that. The Vatican's motto is *Semper Eadem* (always the same) and the Vatican is never therefore capable of fundamental or radical change. Superficially, however, Rome operates in a similar manner to the chameleon. In nations where she is dominant, she is an oppressor; in nations where she is weak, the strategy is to win friends in high places and undermine whatever challenges her supremacy. It is no accident, for example, that on matters relating to the British monarchy or constitutional reform, the media habitually seeks the comment of Lord St John of Fawsley, a devout Roman Catholic who seems to have become the Queen's personal spokesman. The fact that the Supreme Governor of the Church of England is surrounded by such influential Roman Catholics highlights progressive Anglican subjection to the Papacy. There is no formula for compromise; no vision of a mutually acceptable agreement. Protestantism has to be destroyed in its doctrines, and its institutions have to be absorbed into the Church of Rome, because Rome can brook no rivals. Submission to the Papacy is the only acceptable means of reconciliation. If this sounds incredible, the Papacy throughout history bears testimony to this truth.

It is curious that with an ecumenical climate in which it is not supposed to matter which denomination one belongs to, the recent high-profile conversions to Rome of leading politicians and members of the Royal Family have enjoyed huge media attention, as have the conversions of members of the Anglican clergy. It is even more curious that nothing is made of counter-defections; nothing is said of those Roman Catholics who see the true nature of Romanism and move towards the liberating light of seeing the supremacy of Scripture. Of course, to state these things will invite accusations of extremism, bigotry and prejudice, and the Roman propaganda machine will publicise such remarks. Even so, Britain has been preserved from every Roman Catholic onslaught since the Spanish Armada, and its biblical foundations run deep. With leading media players, senior politicians and members of the Royal Family and of the Church of England all professing leanings towards Rome, the permeation of British society by Catholic 'Truth' is ever greater. Leading cardinals have long espoused the strategy. Cardinal Newman observed:

> 'Only through the English Church can you act upon the English nation,' [14]

and Cardinal Wiseman thought pretty much the same:

> 'England must return to Catholic unity through the established church.' [15]

This is certainly being achieved today.

The constant demands for unity among Christians have become a means of silencing criticism. It is no longer acceptable to raise legitimate concerns, because believers are misleadingly exhorted *'to keep the unity of the Spirit in the bond of peace'* (*Ephesians 4:3*). The example of Jesus' prayer *'that they all may be one ... that the world may believe'* (*John 17:21*) is also cited. Anything which appears to upset this pursuit of unity becomes the 'jarring dissonance', and principalities and powers are left to spread their deception unchecked. As the Bible becomes merely a book of stories, and truth becomes a relative, subjective concept, it is easy to lose sight of Paul's forthright teaching on truth and the Spirit of truth, and his means of countering false teachings and unbiblical practices. Those who acted contrary to *'the doctrine which ye have learned'* were to be avoided (*Romans 16:17*), not united with. Christians were to dissociate themselves from those who lived in immorality (*1 Corinthians 5:11*), not absorb them into the Church. Unrepentant heretics were to be rejected (*Titus 3:10*), not welcomed into a fellowship of love, peace and unity. Truth has to go hand-in-hand with unity, or unity has no foundation. When Jesus prayed that they might be one, he had previously prayed:

> '*Sanctify them through thy truth: thy word is truth.*'
> (*John 17:17*)

The doctrines of the Roman Catholic Church have long been proven antithetical to the Word of God, so it should be all the more disturbing that the ascending religious spirit in the United Kingdom is now Roman Catholicism, as it is the dominant State religion of Europe.

## References

1. *The Anatomy of Melancholy*, Robert Burton.
2. *Europe: The Challenge*, EPP Group, December 1983.
3. The *Sunday Telegraph*, August 4th 1991.
4. *Business Agenda for a Free Europe*, European Research Group, London.
5. Brigadier Cowgill, Director, British Management Data Foundation, *Freedom Today*, April 1996.
6. *The Guardian*, 14th June 1996.
7. *The Rotten Heart of Europe*, Bernard Connolly, Faber & Faber, 1995.
8. *Financial Times*, 4th January 1993.
9. *The Rotten Heart of Europe*, Bernard Connolly, Faber & Faber, 1995.
10. *In Their Own Words*, Christopher Gill MP, SEK Publications, 1996.
11. *Ibid.*
12. *Daily Telegraph*, 9th January 1996.
13. *The Rotten Heart of Europe*, Bernard Connolly, Faber & Faber, 1995.
14. *Rome's Strategy for England*, Dr David Samuel, Protestant Truth Society, London.
15. *Ibid.*

# Chapter 10

## The Only Way Forward?

*'There is a way which seemeth right unto a man, but the end thereof are the ways of death.'*     (*Proverbs 14:12*)

Historically, the strength of Europe lay in the stability and inheritance of its nations. Not one single significant achievement in Europe – and certainly not the defeat of German imperialism and national socialism in two world wars – came from supra-national powers. Instead, such achievements came from individual nations acting alone, or from alliances formed between sovereign nations. As a result of Britain's reduced capacity for unilateral actions – through the erosion of sovereignty and the undermining of Parliament's autonomy – Britain now finds itself in a kind of no-man's-land between yesterday and tomorrow. Everyone knows that things cannot continue as at present. A few hope for a solution through a return to the past, and others look for the glorious New World Order.

### A world elsewhere

It was Churchill who said that Britain must find 'ties of blood, sentiment, tradition and common interest' to unite the British family of nations. Those who talk about Britain's 'European destiny' would scoff at such talk, and would overpower rational discussion with threats of being 'left behind' or being handicapped in some 'outer tier' or 'slow lane' or 'left outside' altogether. However, this would hardly be the apocalyptic disaster these doom merchants prophesy. Despite all the restrictions, distortions and handicaps placed by the EU on Britain's trade with the rest of the world, more than half its exports go to countries outside the EU. The strength of Britain's bargaining power in any future negotiations with the EU is considerable, for Britain is a major contributor to the EU budget. Britain is the only net consumer of many of the Union's surplus agricultural products, a major net importer of EU manufacturers, one of the most important providers of fishing waters to the Common Fisheries Policy, and the only country currently self-sufficient in energy. This is hardly a scenario which indicates that the 'only way forward' is pro-Europe. Britain's historic ties, her geo-strategic position straddling the sea-lanes to four continents, and the close economic and cultural links to the great English-speaking democracies of the Atlantic and Pacific basins, all enable far wider interests and connections than simply those to neighbouring continental nations. Since 75 per cent of all Britain's overseas investment lies outside the EU (41 per cent being in the United States alone), there is potential for an eye-opening trade bonanza if 'Little Europeanism' were exchanged for a 'whole world' trade outlook.

The problem with the word 'withdrawal' is that it sounds so final. It is not assisted by the tabloid war-speak on Europe, 'withdrawal' implying defeat and failure. Even so, a heading in *The Times* of 14th June 1996 stated what few prominent Christians and politicians had had the courage to say:

'Britain's withdrawal from the EU need not be suicidal.'

To state this so abruptly is considered eccentric –́ a swimming against the tide – and anyone who dares criticise the workings of Brussels is automatically accused of secretly favouring withdrawal from the Union, as though it were somehow shameful. But as *The Times* observed:

> 'The pursuit by Britain's European partners of deeper integration has placed strains on this country's political, economic and legal systems. That strain may be ... a price worth paying, but it would be practising deceit on the British public not to examine the costs and benefits of membership scrupulously and to consider if there is a worthwhile alternative.'

The ideal option would be for the EU to abandon deeper integration and evolve into a community of nation states, but this looks unlikely while the entire oligarchy – the Commission, Court and Parliament – are designed specifically and bound legally to propel nations towards a single goal: the advancing of political integration. No amount of British vetoing, re-negotiating, or opting out will change the course of 40 years of European integration, a course which is set and enshrined in enforceable treaties. The 'worthwhile alternative', therefore, may be that of leaving the EU altogether. Certainly such a move would be a wrench, but EU propaganda of 'retreating into isolation' needs to be weighed against the advice of many learned economists, politicians and defenders of the British Constitution, who believe such a move could be a liberation and, far from a retreating withdrawal, an entry into a wider world.

There are four possible routes: the 'Norwegian', the 'Swiss', the 'American' and the 'untried':

1. The Norwegian path – membership merely of the European Economic Area – has yielded much in terms of its citizens' standards of living. It provides access to the single market with freedom of movement for goods, services, capital and people, without involvement in the common fisheries or agricultural policies, or any need

to subscribe to shared fiscal, social, foreign or security policies. It does, however, mean the country pays into cohesion funds, and accepts single-market regulations without having the chance to shape them. For Britain, it is possibly one of the poorer deals.

2.  The Swiss option is the simple EFTA bilateral free-trade arrangement with the EU. Switzerland is free to apply EU regulations as it wishes. In some sectors, notably banking, it benefits from not doing so. Trade with the EU has not suffered. Of Switzerland's exports, 63 per cent goes to the EU (compared with only 47 per cent of Britain's). Although Swiss goods can freely enter the EU, Swiss citizens do not enjoy the freedom to work there, a freedom which Britons have, and which any British government would wish to preserve. There is no reason why the EFTA could not be expanded and improved. Then there would be two Europes; the EU – bureaucratic, corporatist and dominated by Germany; and the EFTA – an association of free nations.

3.  The American arrangement is to have no formal link with the EU at all, merely access to markets guaranteed by international agreements. Although outside the single market, the US has, since 1990, increased its exports to the EU faster than Britain has, principally due to the World Trade Organisation's lowering of the EU's external tariff from 5.7 per cent to 3.6 per cent, making market penetration far easier. Although a tariff is still a tariff, and British goods would be subject to such a tariff, it could be less of a burden for business than high social costs imposed by Germany or regulations imposed by Brussels. The remote prospect of a protectionist Europe wreaking revenge on a departing Britain has receded further since the World Trade Organisation was given new powers to make retaliatory action against any recalcitrant bloc easier.

4.  And finally, the untried path. There is no reason at all why Britain should follow any established path. Britain is in a unique position, and has considerable leverage. With the current considerable trade deficit, the other EU members would fight hard to preserve their access to the British market. Moreover, Britain has, under a Conservative government, a veto on the future development of the EU. The implementation of Labour's plans to abandon the veto, permitting the other nations to integrate without hindrance, may be the path to an EU concession for the full freedom of movement of British goods and citizens. An agreement to abandon the veto may therefore be the lever by which sovereignty could be regained: in return for the freedom to go their own way, the federal EU might just concede such freedoms to a sovereign and independent Britain.

Paradoxically, any moves to retrieve sovereignty or assert independence may actually increase Britain's influence in Europe. France wants Britain to share Europe's defence burden and counter-balance Germany, Italy wants an ally to balance the Franco-German axis, and the northern EU states value Britain's financial input and its influence in pressing for liberal economics. All of these nations may be more inclined to accept British arguments if they thought Britain were prepared, if perpetually frustrated, to leave them to each other. But only a sovereign Britain would be free to leave them to each other. The moment of monetary and political union would be irrevocable, and would bind Britain to Europe in perpetuity. Such a move would be an offence to Britain's culture, a rape of Britain's heritage, a corruption of Britain's laws and a perilous surrender of Britain's constitution and democracy. US Republican Presidential contender, Pat Buchanan, commented:

> 'If I were an MP I'd be Euro-sceptic too. How can you let a country with a great history, sovereign for

20 generations, disappear as a province of a bureau-cratic Euro-state run by Helmut Kohl?' [1]

Winston Churchill clarified Britain's best way forward. He observed:

'We are with Europe, but not of it. We are linked, but not combined. We are interested and associated, but not absorbed.' [2]

For all the demands and pleas for Britain to be at the heart of Europe, the stark fact needs reiterating that Britain does not want to be at the heart of Europe if the heart of Europe is diseased.

According to Scripture, there is ultimately only one decision upon which life or death depends – the Way of salvation. All other ways have options, and the arguments in favour of Europe are certainly not as clear cut as the principality or power called Europe might have Britain believe. Just as Churchill called the nation to prayer on the eve of the Battle of Britain, the current threat from the Continent is no less worthy of constant prayer, and the call is just as urgent. It is a righteous government which will restore British sovereignty, pursue righteous laws and maintain the Constitution of liberty which has served Britain for centuries and by which the Gospel can be freely proclaimed. Britain can be restored to her sovereign great-ness, and the Word of God clearly shows the way:

*'Righteousness exalteth a nation.'*     (*Proverbs 13:34*).

### References
1.  *Daily Telegraph*, 8th February 1996.
2.  Winston Churchill, Zurich, Switzerland, 1946.

# Appendix 1

The letter to the Speaker of the House of Commons from the Chairman of the Freedom Association, Norris McWhirter, setting out the case for her intervention in the process to ratify the *Maastricht Treaty*. Published in *Freedom Today*, February 1993:

Dear Madam Speaker,

Although there is no very recent precedent for the Speaker to intervene in debate when the House of Commons is in Committee, it must surely become a duty of the Chair to do so if, on advice, this should be warranted. I refer to the proceedings now being pursued with the intent of ratifying the *Treaty on European Union*, which may be ratified only (per its own article R) in accordance with the respective constitutional requirements of each of the High Contracting Parties.

The conflicts of this treaty with the Law of our Constitution and the Law of Parliament itself appear unparalleled in their number and their brazenness. I would draw some of these to your attention by citing some examples:

1. Constitutionally, no Parliament may bind its successors (see Vauxhall Estates Ltd v. Liverpool Corporation 1932 IKB 733).

Yet the draftsmen of the treaty have (a) omitted any mechanism whatsoever for secession, (b) provided unlimited penalties for non-performance, which can be exacted under Articles 170–171 by the European Court of Justice, and (c) included a clause in Article Q which reads: 'This treaty is concluded for an unlimited period.' In short, any ratification by Parliament would bind its successors, contrary to the Law of our Constitution. This of itself makes ratification inadmissible insofar as it cannot be achieved without essential amendments which are impossible.

2. The Commons have never formally resiled, since it was established, from their exclusive constitutional power of remitting as well as imposing taxation.

   Yet Article 192 of the consolidate draft reaffirms that an external and unelected power would be authorised to impose taxation by usurping Parliament's former monopoly and in a way, and to a degree, however unreasonable or retrospective, that the taxpayer is helpless to resist. Article 192 reads: 'Decisions of the Council or the Commission which impose a pecuniary obligation on persons other than States shall be enforceable.'

3. Article 8b(1) of the treaty seeks to authorise the eligibility of nationals of other EEC nations to stand for election in the municipal elections of the United Kingdom.

   Yet S3 of the Act of Settlement, 1701, precludes all such candidates unless they are naturalised or native citizens (see also Nationality and Status of Aliens Act, 1914).

4. Articles J1–J11 of the treaty seek to authorise a liability of United Kingdom citizens to be called to

serve on a qualified majority vote, i.e. without a British veto.

Yet S3 of the Act of Settlement, 1701, precludes the nation from engaging in any war for the defence of the territories not belonging to the English (now United Kingdom) crown without the specific consent of our Parliament.

5.  Ratification of the treaty would put HM the Queen in breach of her solemn Coronation Oath and thereby be in breach of the Coronation Act, 1953, the terms of which bind her not for part of her reign but for her entire reign. The relevant passage enacted into law reads as follows:

> *Archbishop*: Will you solemnly promise and swear to govern the peoples of the United Kingdom of Great Britain and Northern Ireland ... according to their laws and customs?

> *The Queen*: I solemnly promise to do so.

It cannot be argued that any future laws imposed upon this country by a European parliament in which the United Kingdom has a ceiling of less than 16 per cent of the voting power, could be categorised as 'their laws and customs'. Nor could it have ever been envisaged in 1953 that our Westminster Parliament would seek to subordinate itself to a nine language legislature overseas, which was not then in existence.

6.  The Promissory Oaths Act, 1868, requires all members of Parliament per ss8 and 11 to swear or affirm that they shall be 'faithful and bear true allegiance to Her (Present) Majesty'.

To debate, divide and vote upon a treaty which puts Her Majesty into clear breach of her most solemn oath cannot be reconciled, however ingeniously, with being either 'faithful' or to bearing 'true allegiance'.

Many will feel that if the holder of your office has the undisputed power to check irrelevance in debate, then *a fortiori* she must have the power to check blatant unconstitutionality being debated at all. Furthermore, if the Speaker has and accepts the duty to protect the right of minorities, *a fortiori* she must have the duty to protect the rights of majorities, or indeed the totality of the electorate, on such matters as the diminution of democracy and the superimposing upon Westminster of a superior overseas parliament which cannot be democratically dismissed by the British people.

In addition, the electorate would be unconstitutionally exposed to the levying of taxation and transfers of the nation's and personal wealth to other European countries without any means by which they can lawfully resist. Liability to conscription in foreign wars and profound changes in electoral arrangements, without even the calling of a Speaker's conference, are being attempted with no referendum, as if Parliament were the owner rather than the custodian of the people's rights and liberties. Since Parliament comprises the Sovereign, the Commons, and the House of Lords, and as the presiding officer of the House of Commons, who has a right of access to HM the Queen (who retains the constitutional right to warn), it is hoped and trusted that these matters of ultimate constitutional gravity will receive your most urgent and effective attention with a view, under your own oath as a Privy Councillor, to calling a halt to what is nothing less than a series of unconstitutional and anti-democratic outrages, being promoted by an overseas movement with the compliance of a body which has no legal existence, namely the Cabinet.

The treaty (Article 8) even seeks to impose compulsorily, and without any consultation or approval, upon every British Citizen, the undefined 'duties' of European citizenship.

Article 8 provides for no exception, since it is worded to apply to 'every person holding the nationality of a Member State'. Thus it reduces our Sovereign to becoming a compulsory European citizen who becomes unconstitutionally open to arraignment under the civil and criminal law of the European Community. Superior Community law would not and could not thus even take account of the rule that succeeding Sovereigns are deemed constitutionally never to be infants.

To use the words, though not the context, of a statute still in force, the Bill of Rights, 1688:

> These matters are utterly and directly contrary to the knowne lawes and statutes and freedoms of this realme and that the entire perfect and full exercise of the regall power and government be onely in and executed by His (now Her) Majestie ... And thereunto the said lords spirituall and temporall and commons doe in the name of the people ... and doe promise that they will stand to maintaine and defend their said Majesties (and their heirs) ... with their lives and estates against all persons whatsoever that shall attempt anything to the contrary.'

It is argued that the nation should not be allowed a referendum, even when its constitution is in process of being systematically destroyed, because Britain is a parliamentary democracy. However, the present lamentable Parliament is engaged in an unconstitutional exercise to end parliamentary democracy and even its own significance, together with yours.

Unless the presiding officer of this Parliament acts with the famous resolution and courage of Speaker Brand on 2nd February 1881 in following precedent by terminating debate in Committee upon her own responsibility, this Parliament will deservedly go down in history as the one which was allowed, in total disregard for all constitutional safeguards, to extinguish Britain's self-governance and government by consent, and thereby lay the foundations for the collapse of the rule of law and of the Queen's peace.

# Appendix 2

Generalised table of current VAT within the European Union on sensitive commodities (*Source*: Campaign for an Independent Britain):

| | Food in shops | Children's clothing | Books | News-papers | Public transport | House purchases New | 2nd hand |
|---|---|---|---|---|---|---|---|
| **UK** | **0** | **0** | **0** | **0** | **0** | **0** | **0** |
| Belgium | 6 | 19 | 6 | 6 | 6 | 17 | 0 |
| Denmark | 25 | 25 | 25 | 0 | 0 | 25 | 0 |
| France | 5.5 | 18.6 | 5.5 | 2.1 | 5.5 | 18.6 | 0 |
| Germany | 7 | 14 | 7 | 7 | 7, 14 | 0 | 0 |
| Greece | 8 | 18 | 4 | 4 | 8 | 4–36 | 0 |
| Ireland | 0 | 12.5 | 0 | 10 | 0 | 10 | 0 |
| Italy | 4–12 | 19 | 4 | 4 | 0, 9 | 4, 19 | 4, 19 |
| Luxembourg | 3, 6 | 15 | 6 | 6 | 6 | 0 | 0 |
| Netherlands | 6 | 18.5 | 6 | 6 | 6 | 18.5 | 0 |
| Portugal | 0, 8(6) | 17 | 0 | 0 | 8 | 0 | 0 |
| Spain | 6 | 13 | 6 | 6 | 6 | 13(6) | 0 |

# Appendix 3

The Cost of Brussels over three years (Figures courtesy of HM Government, quoted in *Freedom Today*, the journal of the Freedom Association):

|                      | 1993 | 1994 | 1995 | Total |
|----------------------|------|------|------|-------|
| Payments             | 8.0  | 7.2  | 8.9  | 24.1  |
| Receipts             | 5.8  | 5.1  | 4.8  | 15.7  |
| **UK Net contribution** | **2.1** | **2.1** | **4.1** | **8.3** |

*Note*: Amounts are expressed in £billions.

As receipts from Brussels are shrinking, payments increase, doubling the UK's net contribution in 1995 compared with 1994. This, of course, is in addition to the massive trade deficit which the UK has with the other EU countries.